Very Nearly Me

Adventures of an Anglophile

Evelyn Copeland

DORRANCE PUBLISHING CO., INC.
PITTSBURGH, PENNSYLVANIA 15222

Other books by Evelyn Copeland
But a Brown Bird Sang
Lonesome Glee: Tales from the Birding Trails
"*Susie*" (unpublished)

ISBN # 0-8059-6656-0
Printed in the United States of America

First Printing

For information or to order additional books, please write:
Dorrance Publishing Co., Inc.
701 Smithfield Street
Third Floor
Pittsburgh, Pennsylvania 15222-3906
U.S.A.
1-800-788-7654
Or visit our web site and on-line catalog at www.dorrancepublishing.com

For Virginia (Ginny) Dearborn,
who shared my love for Great Britain, its land and its people.

Contents

Preface

THIS MEMOIR OF SORTS has been simmering on the back burner for many years. The time has come, I believe, to tender the world a tender sampling or else throw the ragout out. Chronologically it is a thin slice of a wide variety of folks I met in the mid-thirties—my mid-thirties. Some I met briefly under exceptional circumstances. Others became friends for life, leaving deep footprints on my heart. All have had a part in creating the me I have come to be.

Nor is this even a complete serving. The Hatleys, for instance, deserve a chapter of their own. I met Mrs. Hatley on a city bus in Exeter early in my travels around Great Britain. She invited me to walk with her to Hardy's birthplace when I came to Dorchester and to meet her family—husband, two daughters, grandsons, and neighbors, the Poveys. One of the Povey daughters spent a Christmas holiday with my family and me in Connecticut. And more importantly, the Hatleys shared a Christmas with me when I was alone and just a wee bit home sick in England.

Lady Wylie, widow of Lord Wylie who headed the Rhodes Scholar program in Oxford, deserves her own chapter, too. By the luck of the draw she was my cabin mate when I crossed the Atlantic on the Queen Mary in 1954. It was she who introduced me to the Archbishop of York and his wife on shipboard. She also kept in touch and entertained me in her home while I was living in Oxford and later after I moved to London.

Helen Layton shared her home with me for six weeks in Oxford. She and her housemate, the inimitable Mrs. Sherwood-Smith, made me one of the family. The cuisine was delicious, the ambience gracious, and the conversation always stimulating. I noted in my diary the first day I met Mrs. Sherwood-Smith, "she fixes me with a cool eye and one raised eyebrow, has an idea or two…no trite expression or platitudes will do here." Mrs. Sherwood-Smith believed in ghosts, as do I, and had met a few she enjoyed recalling for me.

Then there was the weekend with my namesakes, Gresham and Spencer Copeland and their families in their homes and at the Copeland-Spode porcelain factory in Stoke-on-Trent. The list goes on and on. Some of these folks are bound to turn up in later slices of my life. Let chronology fall where it will. All in all this is a memoir of a remarkable experience.

One last note: the Winnie-the-Poohish title was a gift from a friend renowned for her quick wit and repartee. It preceded the book by several years. I regret she did not live to critique the manuscript.

Evelyn Copeland
Southbury CT 06488
October 29, 2003

Acknowledgments

I thank John Jayne, who unceasingly sought the source of Emily Bronte's "I battled against the rain today;" Carol Miller, who taught me the ways of my wayward computer; and Florence McDermott, who happily performed the household chores while I composed the manuscript. I am greatly indebted, also, to the journals I have kept through the years and without which the current book would lack many specifics of places, times, and menus.

Further, I acknowledge the following sources of quoted materials:
Lines from Macbeth, The Portable Shakespeare, The Penguin Group, (USA) Inc., 1977.

"I had often wished to see..." Charlotte Bronte from A Springtime Saunter around Bronte Land, by Whitely Turner, Halifax Courier, 1913.

"I have seen the dell..." Emily Bronte in The Complete Poems of Emily Jane Bronte, C.W. Hatfield, ed., Columbia University Press, 1995.

Lines from "To a Mouse," Robert Burns from Oxford Book of English Verse, Christopher Ricks, ed., 1999.

"I'm Nobody!" Emily Dickinson from The New Modern American and British Poetry, Louis Untermeyer, ed., Global Rights Group, 1962.

"I have loved England," Alice Duer Miller from White Cliffs, Coward-McCann, 1940.

"Dover Beach," Matthew Arnold from Oxford Book of English Verse, Christopher Ricks, ed., 1999.

"Only a man harrowing clods...," Thomas Hardy from a personally taped unrestricted reading of Hardy's poems by Gertrude Bugler.

Lines from Snoebjorn Jonsson's "Gertrude Bugler," and Florence Hardy's Christmas letter December, 1920, were furnished by Gertrude Bugler, the subject of the chapter "Hardy's Own Tess."

Bard of Avon

SUMMER SCHOOL, STRATFORD-UPON-AVON, the bulletin in my mailbox said. Offered by University of Birmingham. Subject: William Shakespeare. An attached note queried, Interested? It could have come from only one source, a friend and colleague in the English department.

Not impulsive by nature, I replied, a few days later, Maybe.

But within the month we had both applied and were both accepted for summer school in Stratford-upon-Avon. The excitement grew. I was the first in my family to cross the Atlantic Ocean since my "many times" great-grandfather came from England to America in the seventeenth century. This was now 1953.

Winnie and I booked on the Brittanic, which had served as a troop ship during the recent war but had now been reconverted for passenger service. We would return at the end of the summer on the Georgic, another Cunard vessel that had served in the war. Neither was luxurious, but we had nothing with which to compare them.

The Brittanic did give me the thrill of a storm at sea. With the permission of a sailor standing nearby—whether he had authority to give such permission I did not ask—I had taken several tentative steps up a ladder rising from the third-class deck when the ship hit the first great roll of a storm that had been pending. Suddenly I was looking straight down into the ocean. Tightening my grasp on the camera as well as the rung of the ladder, I made a cautious retreat to the deck and stumbled to the nearest chair. Only a smattering of passengers remained outside, braving the winds to watch the storm grow.

The quickly assembled crew stashed chairs haphazardly out of the wind. The ocean roiled, the clouds burst, and the last of the landlubbers groped for handrails as they staggered inside. Tea was not served on deck that afternoon. The dining room was relatively empty that evening. However, I was there with a moderately good appetite. That was more than I could claim a year later when I crossed from New Castle to Bergen, Norway. I am not immune to mal de mer. The little green monster has attacked me in a rowboat in Long Island Sound and has found me during a birding expedition on the Outer Banks of North Carolina and as far south as Deception Bay in Antarctica. But I sailed blithely through this challenge in mid-Atlantic. Pale, perhaps, but unscathed.

Precautions were taken in the dining room to assure the cutlery and dishes did not go sailing into space. Hinged strips of wood hanging on the sides of the dining table were turned up, making a protective edge. Later in my upper berth I felt truly rocked in the cradle of the deep. By morning the sea had calmed.

The Brittanic docked in Liverpool. With a week at our disposal before summer school began, we explored Liverpool and nearby Chester and picked up a few British phrases, such as dead slow, which I gathered meant as slow as one can go and still keep moving. A guest in a bed-and-breakfast inn told us of an American who when asked how far he had traveled up the Mersey River that day, replied, "As far as Dead Slow." I might have made the same mistake if I had not previously heard of such villages as Careless End, Lurking Hope, Guzzle Down, Mousehole (pronounced Moozle), or Snettishham—all villages in Great Britain. The latter, not far from Sandringham in Norfolk, the country home of the royal family, is pronounced Sneez'em.

With still a few days to spare, we rented a car and drove to the Lake District. My first impression was that it could as well be called the Mountain District. The scenery was exhilarating; the weather, warm. One afternoon as we were climbing around Bassenthwaite, north of Keswick, with Skiddaw's three-thousand-foot peak beckoning, I began to regret I had not kept my bathing suit out when I forwarded my luggage to Stratford. The idea of swimming occurred to us a few miles out of Keswick when we came upon a secluded cove in a small lake, more of a pond really. Some cows stood knee deep at one edge in the shade of the bordering trees.

"Lucky cows," Winnie said.

"If they can, why can't we?" I countered. We parked the car and strolled on through the trees until we were out of sight of cars and road. Seeing no sign of human life, we disrobed and waded in sans suits, splashing around like happy tadpoles.

When we arrived a few days later at the Wayside Inn in Stratford-upon-Avon, where the summer school had found a home for us, the host greeted us with, "The police were here looking for you yesterday." Surely, I thought, news of our swimming in the nude could not travel this far this fast. Actually, one of my suitcases had been broken into in transit, and the police wanted to know whether anything was missing. As far as I could ascertain nothing had been taken.

The Wayside Inn was a small bed-and-breakfast inn run by a Mr. and Mrs. Jones, where a few of the international students were housed for the six-week Shakespeare course. The other half of the inn was reserved for transients, giving us an opportunity each evening in the lounge to meet some Brits, often on holiday. That was true of the Reverend Jones and his wife, who invited Winnie and me to spend a weekend with them at their home in Holyhead, Wales, after summer school ended. And we accepted. Holyhead is a splotch on a headland that extends miles into the Irish Sea on a northwest jog of the Welsh coast. It was a weekend to remember for both hospitality and scenery. That, however, is another story.

The six-week course in Shakespeare was leisurely, open-ended, and stimulating. At ten o'clock five mornings a week, a Shakespearean professor or scholar (often but not exclusively from the faculty of the University of Birmingham) lectured on the Bard, his plays, his life and environment, his contemporaries, or his critics. Frequently the lecture had a built-in itinerary for a self-directed adventure in the afternoon.

The Wayside Inn was within easy walking distance of all the places most intimately connected with Shakespeare—Mary Arden's Farm where he was born; a weekly market similar to what he as a young lad doubtlessly attended with his father; the Guild Hall Grammar School, where he learned his "little Latin and less Greek"; the Knott Gardens at New Place; the home he built when he returned from his years in London; Hall's Croft where his daughter and her physician husband lived very comfortably. Unlike New Place, which a later owner—annoyed by persistent tourists wanting to see the house—tore down, Hall's Croft still stood, open to the public. One could see there not only the living quarters but also the dispensary, equipped with pestle and mortar, scales and vials, and such of the day. The gardens in both of the latter were riots of color all summer.

In the course of six weeks, we had opportunities to see all the plays being performed at the Shakespeare Memorial Theatre on the banks of the Avon that summer. Between the Theatre and Clopton Bridge, which crosses the Avon, were the Bancroft Gardens, also bordering the river. A large statue of Shakespeare in the center of the gardens was encircled by four smaller ones, representing Lady Macbeth, Hamlet, King Lear, and Henry V. At any hour, tourists from many countries, in sunshine or in rain, could be seen gazing at the statues, admiring the flowers, resting on a bench, strolling along the river, lounging on the grass, or invariably taking photographs. Swans glided silently up and down the river; willows grew along its banks. I spotted one willow whose lower branch stretched horizontally aslant the brook. I'm sure it was the one from which Ophelia slipped and drowned among her garlands. Just to the south of the theater, and also on the banks of the Avon, is Holy Trinity Church. The Geraert Janssen memorial bust, erected in 1660, marks Shakespeare's tomb with the epitaph warning "and curst be he who moves these bones." The warning has been observed for nearly three and a half centuries and doubtlessly will be for the foreseeable future. Stratford for the most part had been spared the bombs of World War II. Though the devastation of the war was still all too evident around Britain, the recent coronation of Elizabeth II, we found, with all its pomp and circumstance, had buoyed the British spirit.

In addition to several British members of the morning class, we were fortunate to meet on one occasion or another a number of other Stratfordites eager to host the foreign visitors. Out of nowhere Mrs. Cuthbert appeared the second day in her Jaguar to take Winnie and me to lunch at the Black Swan. We saw no special reason she selected us, and we did not see much of her again. Miss Ralston, on the other hand, turned up again and again. She was a font of Shakespeare lore and made sure we visited places like the Shakespeare Hotel, for instance. Of Tudor design it stands on the principal street in a row of Tudor buildings that includes the grammar school.

"Nearly four hundred years ago little William Shakespeare passed this house of Sir Hugh Clopton, " Miss Ralston told us, "on his way to school each day." The "Great House," as it was then known was one of the finest houses in Stratford-upon-Avon. Today it is operated by Trust Houses Limited, the largest privately owned hotel group in Great Britain, not government-owned and not to be confused with the National Trust.

"That must be the same Sir Clopton for whom Clopton Bridge is named," I observed.

"You are right," Miss Ralston agreed, "and I want you to go inside the hotel now to see how the rooms are named."

Inside we found each room bore the title of a Shakespearean play. One might spend the night in Love's Labour Lost or A Midsummer's Night Dream, All's Well That Ends Well, or Taming of the Shrew. The possibilities of The Tempest especially stirred my imagination. She also made sure we walked the short distance through the fields to Shottery to visit Anne Hathaway's cottage.

I found another friend in Mr. Holte, who owned and ran the photography shop in Stratford. The majority of my pictures were Kodak slides, but I had another little camera that took square pictures in black and white. I had dreams of taking one black and white so spectacular that I could have it enlarged and hung on the wall of a home that was still another part of the dream. A cathedral would be appropriate, I thought. To that end I visited a number of cathedrals with that in mind. I could not get far enough away from St. Paul's for an effective shot. Winchester didn't speak to me, but when I saw Salisbury Cathedral, I knew I had found what I was looking for. Alas though, I could not get far enough away to get that lovely, delicate spire entirely within my viewfinder. Drat! I thought. I sat on a bench, admiring the graceful lines, when the solution came to me. Since the picture would be square, why not turn the camera forty-five degrees? That brought the spire into a corner, not an edge, of the picture. What's more I could get the whole spire, blue sky and all, into the frame. I belabor this incident a bit because Mr. Holte made such a point of my solution when he developed the picture. I felt I had really made a friend.

Salisbury Cathedral

Each morning we had a ten- to fifteen-minute break during the ninety-minute lectures. During one of these breaks a man invited me to have a cuppa with him after the session. He introduced himself as Harry Clark, local citizen. Over coffee I learned he was the director of a gigantic pageant in the process of being mounted for presentation at Warwick Castle later in the summer. The pageant would celebrate a visit of Queen Elizabeth I to the Castle. Harry made sure that Winnie and I had tickets for opening night and transportation to Warwick, a half-hour's drive north of Stratford. The performance started about sunset under a clear sky. Pink and purple sunset clouds lined the horizon. Floodlights lit the ramparts of the castle. There, for over two hours, hundreds of spectators relived seventeenth-century history, climaxing with the arrival of Queen Elizabeth and her entourage on snow-white horses. When Sir Walter Raleigh with his own attendants emerged from the castle to meet her, a collective gasp swept across the assembled spectators. What a spectacular production it was!

Well, summer school in Stratford-upon-Avon ended all too soon, and I knew before I disembarked from the Georgic that I must find a way to return soon to Great Britain. Before the end of the next school year I had applied for and been awarded a Ford Fellowship for individual study abroad. My school board, bless them, granted me a year's leave of absence, and on August 25, 1954, after the call "All ashore who are going ashore," I stood on deck of the Queen Mary, waving my waving flag to Mom and Dad, sister, nephews, cousins, friends, and friends of friends. As the Barbara Dorin and Doris Morin tugged the Mary's nose eastward, the thunderstorm, which had been threatening, let go one terrific crash. I felt appropriately launched.

I disembarked six days later in Southampton and took the next boat train to London. My first stop was at the English-Speaking Union. I felt at home on the London tubes but suddenly terribly alone in a big city. Whatever had I been thinking when I applied for that fellowship! I was happy to find mail waiting for me, a letter from a student and a note from Marjorie and Eleanor. The latter were friends who had been vacationing in Switzerland. They would be flying into London that afternoon. The note suggested dinner at their hotel.

Inspired by this contact with friends and having four hours on my hands, I went out and bought a car, at least ordered one to be delivered to me in Edinburgh the next week. That done I made a trip to the American Express for a check certifying that the funds for the car had originated outside England, a trip back to the English-Speaking Union for a letter confirming that I intended to leave the country within a year, and a trip to a Customs Office to swear on oath I would export the car. That left me just time to walk through Hyde Park to White's Hotel at Lancaster Gate to meet Marge and Eleanor for dinner. I believed the evening paper when it reported this the hottest day of the summer.

I had earlier exchanged my reservation on the Flying Scotsman for a sleeper and so I left my friends at nine to pick up my bags at "left luggage" and catch the train at Kings Cross for a ten o'clock departure. By 10:15 I was in my bunk massaging aching feet and soon asleep.

Edinburgh was my first port of call because I wanted to see its renowned Military Tattoo. After that I would continue the previous summer's pursuit of Shakespeare by visiting all the Scottish places named in Macbeth. Except for his historical plays, Macbeth is the most British of all Shakespeare's plays. Whether Shakespeare himself ever visited the places he mentions in the play is questionable. He could have written the play with a minimal knowledge of history and a good map. But what a wonderful excuse I had for traipsing around Scotland and meeting Scottish folk.

After breakfast at the station café, I took a taxi to 22 Dundas Street and Miss Kenneth, with whom I had a reservation for a minimum of two weeks. She was a bit startled to see me at her door at 8:30 in the morning but recovered her composure quickly. Skipping and leaping, she led me up the sixty-seven steps to the fourth-floor (by American count) tiny bedroom and large living room that were to be mine as long as I wanted. The mattress, it turned out, was remarkably lumpy, but who cared? Obviously not Miss Kenneth. After some unpacking I went out to sniff the city.

Afternoon found me back at the Waverly Station to meet Bessie Jennings, a colleague of mine from home. She had just arrived from Newcastle-on-Tyne, having spent the night on the Bergen-Newcastle ferry. I went along to her hotel where a cousin from Glasgow soon joined us for tea. A little later Jean Bain, a Scottish art teacher who was once an exchange teacher in the school where Bessie and I taught, met us. We all piled onto tram #23, which took us up the hill to the Military Tattoo on the Esplanade of the Edinburgh Castle.

Miss Kenneth and I established 9:00 A.M. as my breakfast hour. Mr. Foster, an elderly transient guest, ate at 8:30, and she thought I would not enjoy him. After a little more settling in—though my suitcase and footlocker sent as unaccompanied luggage on my train ticket, had not yet arrived—I left for Freemason's Hall for a morning concert by the Collegium Musicum of Zurich—all string music with a trio of flutes in the third piece. Paul Sacher conducted. Handel's Concerto Grosso in A Minor and Purcell's Sonata No. 6 floated through sighing semiquavers and polyphonic strands, and Willy Burkhard's Concerto for Two Flutes was exciting because he had dedicated it to Paul Sacher's orchestra and this was the first public performance. Willy Burkhard was in the audience and took his bows graciously at the conclusion. But it was Mozart's Divertimento in D Major, K136, that really gave me palpitations. I resolved to get my own recording very soon.

Miss Kenneth was having a roast beef dinner for two friends and suggested I come home for dinner at 12:30. I did. Miss K makes good Yorkshire pudding.

That afternoon I presented myself to the department for aliens, firearms, and dangerous drugs and started procedures for registering my existence in Great Britain. After four signatures and a fee of two-shillings sixpence, I was told I could pick up my identification booklet in a week.

In the meantime Marjorie and Eleanor had arrived in Edinburgh, first to see the Military Tattoo and secondly to accompany me for a day or two as I set out on my pursuit of Macbeth. I met them for supper at their hotel but had to bang right away as Miss Kenneth would say to Macbeth, which was playing at a theater on Princess Street. A few days later, having seen the Tattoo three times and the play once, I was ready to venture forth. Hence, the next morning found the three of us on the 7:40 train for Inverness and Nairn. I kept my room on Dundas Street, assuring Miss Kenneth I would return within the week.

We shared the six-passenger compartment with a couple of young hikers and an older woman on her way to the Pitlochary Drama Festival. One of the hikers seemed to know a great deal about flowers and shrubs as well as the geography of Scotland. As the train wound its way through beautiful mountains spotted with heather and sheep, our young companion pointed out and identified many other examples of the bountiful flora. Later the conversation turned to Scottish words. And he recalled an American hiker who, upon reading the sign, THROW WASH WATER IN BURN, threw it into the fire instead of the stream. He also recommended Inverness over Nairn. There would be more to do in Inverness. I did not take time to explain that my goal was Cawdor Castle, not sightseeing.

When a dining car was attached at Perth, Marge, Eleanor, and I took tickets for the first sitting for breakfast. We sat shivering and obscuring the view with our own breath, but the rolls were delicious and the sun warm once we left the station. Most of the passengers left the train in Inverness, but we continued as planned to Nairn, where we were the only ones to disembark. The Nairn station looked mightily deserted after the train left. As we stood alone looking at each other with a kind of what do we do now look, a lone taxi pulled up. Rather than recommend a hotel, the driver said he would drive us past the hotels along the shore and we could select our own. That is how we came to be in the Royal Marine the next three nights. I was startled for a moment the first night when my toes struck a crockery hot water bottle as I stuck my feet under the bedclothes. I debated whether to sleep with the creature or not and decided not since the bed was now warm and I did not want to break a toe accidentally after going to sleep. I found in the morning that Marge and Eleanor had made the same decision.

Shakespeare himself may never have visited Cawdor Castle, but early in the play when Macbeth meets the witches on the blasted heath, they greet him as Thane of Cawdor. The audience knows but he does not that he is about to become Thane of Cawdor, and therein lies the motivation of a plot waiting to be unraveled. This seemed as good a place as any for me to start visiting places with literary connections. Since a family lived in the castle, I had to apply to the Cawdor estate office in town for permission to visit. Luck was not entirely with me, for the family was at the moment in residence. But at least I wangled permission to walk about the grounds and take pictures.

Though the weather was not promising the next morning, I decided, along with Marge and Eleanor, to go in search of Cawdor. On our way to the bus (my car had not yet arrived), we bought some biscuits, cheese, and fruit in anticipation of a picnic. The bus deposited us at the foot of a long, neatly trimmed driveway marked "To Cawdor Castle: Private." With permission in hand we proceeded, following the drive to a narrow bridge across a burn leading to the village of Cawdor. A little farther we crossed the burn again and soon found ourselves on the grounds of the castle. I tiptoed about, snapping pictures of the drawbridge over the moat, the castle, and the coat of arms above the windows. About that time a spit and polished limousine with chauffeur approached the drawbridge. I so wanted to take a picture of the young lad in red jacket who stepped out and crossed the footbridge, looking very much at home, but the opportunity was lost while I debated whether that would be too, too intrusive. We were not close enough to speak.

Marge, Eleanor, and I continued farther up the woodland path to have our lunch in Cawdor Forest. The drizzle started before we finished our biscuits and cheese. Marge made some comment about "we three witches." Out came my camera and tripod. I set the camera on TIME and ran to join them in the picture, our rain hoods helping us to look the part. Click! Right on cue Marge cackled,

"When shall we three meet again
In thunder, lightning or in rain?"

Eleanor followed up with a wonderfully crackley, witch-like voice,

"When the hurly-burly's done,
When the battle's lost or won."

I completed the opening lines with

"That will be ere the set of sun."

Complimenting ourselves on our sterling performance, we continued our picnic lunch despite the raindrops that drummed a light tattoo upon our rain hoods.

Three witches in Cawdor Forest

The next day Marge and Eleanor felt they must continue with their itinerary, and so we parted, they to Skye and I to the blasted heath, where a picture of the three witches would have had a more authentic setting than yesterday's.

Still with no car, I took the low road by bus to Forres and Aberdeen. In Shakespeare's play the king's palace is in Forres. Banquo asks, as he and Macbeth return from battle, "How far is't called to Forres?" But before they reach Forres, they are waylaid by the witches and their prophecies for Macbeth and Banquo. The driver of the bus had her doubts about the exact locality of Macbeth's Hillock, which I pointed out on my ordnance map. This was not an official bus stop. Nevertheless, I dismounted. Having no idea where I was or when another bus would come along, I gazed at the barrenness surrounding me. As I stood calculating my next move, a woman came out of the toll house, the only habitation within sight. Though some distance up the road, she motioned me toward her. As I approached, she stated more than queried, "You've come to see the hillock?" It is on her property and I was welcome to walk through the bogs and heather to see it. But first Mrs. MacIntosh was eager to talk.

I could see she did not live where neighbors were likely to drop in for tea or to borrow a cup of sugar. She has four sons, she told me. One was a factor on a neighboring estate. Her husband was a gardener in his sixties. They make their own electricity by means of a windmill but had to walk some distance to fetch the water. She had a large garden that did not look as though it wanted for water. In the flower garden were sweet peas (perennials), garden thistles, yellow creeper, purple michaelmas daisies, white heather, and gladioli. On beyond were turnips, cabbages, potatoes, carrots, and beets. White leghorn chickens were running free. It was a very active place here in the middle of the desolate heath.

The MacIntoshes had lived here eight years. Former owners, employees of nearby Brodie Castle, had planted a rowan tree (mountain ash or "rodden") before their baby was born to keep the witches away. That tree now dominates the garden. Young Lord Brodie recently sponsored a local talent show including a take-off on Macbeth. "How far is't to Forres?" "2d. on the bus."

From the hillock one can see Nelson's Tower in Forres on a clear day, she told me. And with that information I decided it was time to have a look for myself. Thanking her for all the information, I bid adieu and set out through the bogs. Macbeth's Hillock, not more than a quarter of a mile beyond the gardens, rose perhaps three or five feet above the flat heath. It was completely covered with bracken except for a small grassy spot maybe five or six feet in diameter on the very top. Some say the witches' cauldron is buried on the hillock, but Mrs. MacIntosh would not vouch for that. I took pictures and stood for a while picturing Macbeth trudging toward Forres and King Duncan's palace to report on the battle just fought. Right where I was standing one witch had greeted him "All hail, Macbeth, that shalt be king hereafter!" I imagined recreating the scene for a class of juniors when I returned to teaching next year.

Back on the highway again, I took the next bus to Forres and from there the train to Aberdeen. The Braemar Highland Gathering was taking place the next day. Being so close, I had decided to attend the games, and so in Aberdeen

I changed for Ballater. Mill of Inver, where I had reservations for the next two nights, was ten miles farther by bus through a land of long-haired Highland cattle, deer, salmon, and rabbits. The woman driving the bus threw newspapers now and then from the bus door and left an occasional package beside the road. A girl with a bundle of firewood and a boy with a large milk can were two of the passengers. Eventually she stopped the bus, looked back at me and said, "This is the Mill of Inver, ma'am."

I disembarked, looked at the retreating bus, inspected the modest, rustic house, and said to myself, "This is really Scotland."

The Mill of Inver had two guests besides me that evening. The other two, Mr. and Mrs. Farnaman, were from Hartford, Connecticut. So I wasn't as completely cut off from home as I had thought. Yesterday's paper had said that chalk and cheese could not be more dissimilar than certain members of the Labor Party. I felt the same could be said of the Royal Marine Hotel in Nairn and the Mill of Inver in Braemar. Here I felt I had left the tourists far behind and been welcomed into the private home of Mr. and Mrs. Wyness. He was a beater or ghillie for the royal shooting parties this time of year. For supper the Farnamans and I were treated to a casserole dish of fried sole, the sole having been fried over the open kitchen fireplace, and home-baked bread with Scottish pancakes for dessert.

Everything was immaculately neat. I do not know where the Farnamans slept, and I'm not quite sure where I slept. I was tempted to call it the pantry because along one side of the narrow room were shelves of homemade jellies and jams. The cot was comfortable enough, and I had room on the floor for my satchel. In my hallway bath was a new cake of milk of sulphur soap, a pitcher of cold water, and a glass of drinking water. The Elsan chemical one-holer in the back yard was neatly papered with pink roses. A carefully trimmed kerosene lamp with matches stood on a triangular shelf beside the cot should I need to venture forth in the night.

Twenty thousand people gathered the next morning in the rain to observe the Braemar Highland Gathering. Once I took my place on the open bleachers, I did not leave it for nearly seven hours. I ate my sandwiches between showers, for the best way to keep dry seemed to be to stay huddled under my rain hood. There were races and hammer throwing, dances, and piping. The bag piping never ceased, individually and in massed pipes and drums. I watched caber throwing and Cumberland wrestling and a tug of war between the Black Watch and the Gordons. But I suspect it was the queen who brought the crowds. The royal party arrived about three o'clock in a brief flash of sunshine, Elizabeth and Philip, the Queen Mother, Princess Margaret, Duchess of Gloucester and her two sons in the midst of massed pipes and "God Save the Queen."

When she left at 4:30, the crowd began to disperse. I rode back to the Mill of Inver with the Farnamans to supper of mealy sausages in cheese sauce, pound cake and jam, and scones. Good food with good conversation by fireplace firelight. Then to sleep with bagpipes ringing in my ears.

After scrambled eggs and sausages the next morning, I said goodbye to Mrs. Wyness. Two of her grandchildren plus two girls who were hiking through Scotland and I climbed aboard the 9:20 bus to Ballater. We caught glimpses of Balmoral through the trees as we departed. I wondered as we rattled along what the queen was having for breakfast and hoped she had not caught cold in the rain yesterday. The grandchildren got off at the schoolhouse and I at the train station. The hikers were going on to the Huntley road where they hoped to find a lorry headed for Inverness. Hitchhiking on lorries seemed to be a popular and safe mode of travel for young people in Scotland.

I had time before my train left to purchase photos of the royal party at the games yesterday. Then I was off to Aberdeen via Dinnet, Aboyne, Dess, Lumphanan, Torphins, and Banchory. I must go back to Lumphanan someday after I get my car. I am told there is much to see and climb. It is another place where Macbeth was really slain. Like George Washington who slept in countless places, devotees of Macbeth lay claim to more than one spot where he was slain. Lumphanan also has a Macbeth Arms Hotel and Macbeth's well. He would be thirsty after all day on the battle field. In Aberdeen I changed to the Edinburgh train and enjoyed a pretty ride home along the coast, across the Tay, and along the Forth. I heard numerous jokes about the frugality for which the Scots are renowned. One was that because of the tradition of throwing out coins for good luck when crossing the Forth, Scots stood below the bridge with inverted umbrellas to catch them. During my visit to Edinburgh, I had many occasions to cross the Firth of Forth by bus, train, and car, and never did I see anyone with an inverted umbrella.

I reached Dundas Street in time to have tea with Miss Kenneth and Eileen Meade, a guest from Liverpool. We talked until 2 A.M. about music, God, and royalty. Miss Meade claimed to be a whalebone conservatist "like all British and can't help it." She nearly came to blows with Miss Kenneth on views concerning royalty. The discussion was fresh in my mind on Sunday when Jean Bain and I took the bus from St. Andrew's Square to the famed Rosslyn Chapel. When we arrived an hour before the service the gate was locked, so we strolled down around Rosslyn Castle, subject of one of Wordsworth's poems, "To Fair Rosslyn." A building between the castle and the chapel bears a plaque indicating that Samuel Johnson, Boswell, Scott, Burns, and Wordsworth had all been entertained there. Back at the chapel the minister in flowing gown and mortared cap arrived, as did the Earl of Rosslyn, two or three women, and a young choirboy. Still the gate was locked. Together the minister and the earl helped the boy over the gate. He found a key and admitted us—thirty-one in the congregation, nine in the choir. After Friday night's interplay between Miss Kenneth and Miss Meade, I wondered whether it was significant that the prayers for the royal family were omitted from the Church of Scotland service that morning.

The Apprentice Pillar in the Rosslyn Chapel is an unusual example of church architecture. The intricate carving, of Portuguese influence, is unique in all of Scotland. It was currently being cleaned, a slow, arduous procedure, and had made headlines recently when workmen found rosaries hidden inside some of the carvings. I did not learn whether Sherlock Holmes had been put onto the case.

• • •

Monday dawned too pleasant a day to spend in museums. So I called Mr. Underwood at Westfield Motors on Lothian Road to ask when I might expect my new car. He had told me earlier that he would take care of registering, insuring, and delivering my Morris Minor once it arrived in Edinburgh. He would enroll me in the Automobile Club, too, for a slight fee. I was excited to hear the car would be ready for me to pick up after three o'clock the next day. When I presented myself the next afternoon, it was waiting—birch gray with red hide upholstery and electric screen wipers that were immediately put to work after I had signed all the documents. Mr. Underwood rode around a block or two with me to see that I could reverse, manage four gears forward, control signal lights, and cope with driving on the left hand side of the road. I could. Once turned loose I was headed straight for Princess Street. My game plan was just to follow the car ahead until I had a chance to turn left off Princess. At George Street another deluge bucketed. I pulled into the next parking spot and read all the literature about tire inflations, gas tank capacity, and oil changes until the sun came out.

My first trial run was out to Queensferry, chiefly because it is a straight, open road but also because I wanted to have tea at Hawes Inn, site of the kidnapping of David Balfour in Robert Louis Stevenson's Kidnapped. The most exciting thing, though, turned out to be the raging Firth of Forth. Waves were pounding over the sea wall and flooding the road. Ferries were tossing about, having a bad time tying up. I had tea in Hawes Inn at a table where I could watch the excitement. The trip back to Dundas Street was uneventful except that I drove the length of one empty (fortunately) side street on the right-hand side. Put the car in a garage conveniently close to my bed and board and dreamed of the places the little gray bug would take me.

The paper next morning said the storm had been frightful in southern England. One man was killed by a falling tree. The Cambridge-London Road had been blocked by fallen trees. Hurricane Edna must have made a five-day trip across the Atlantic. Though still windy in Edinburgh, the blue sky, white clouds, and good visibility bode well for my drive to the Border Country. Miss Kenneth was eager to go as my guide. I drove out of the city, chanting constantly "Keep to the left! Keep to the left" until I got the hang of it. I asked Miss

K whether she was anxious about riding with me. She said she was not. As I have suspected, it takes quite a bit to daunt her. I have tried to think how to describe her, but she defies description. She is first of all energetic. If she were a color, she would be brown—a kind of medium brown; if an animal, a kangaroo. She was mid-fiftyish, uninhibited, well informed, and a rock bottom Scot.

We drove that day through Dalkeith and Lauder to Bemersyde, home of the Haigs of Lady Haig's Poppy Factory and of Field Marshal Earl Haig. Centuries ago Thomas the Rhymer wrote of the Haig family,

> Tyde what may betyde
> Haig will be Haig of Bemersyde.

Or, as one version concludes, "There'll always be a Haig at Bemersyde."

We found the spot called Scott's View, the spot where Sir Walter Scott, Miss Kenneth said, always stopped his horse when returning to Abbottsford to admire the view. I admired it too, looking down into a horseshoe bend of the River Tweed, a nestled farm, three humps of hills in the distance with rolling fields and pastures to the right. About a mile beyond was Dryburgh Abbey. Legend says that when the horses bearing Scott's body from Abbotsford to Dryburgh Abbey came to his view, they stopped as was their custom. At Dryburgh Abbey we found the Haigs and Scotts lying side by side.

I had two more incidents to check out in Macbeth before I left Scotland and decided to get about it now that I had my car. First, to Scone. After King Duncan is murdered, Ross comments,

> ...'tis most like
> The sovereignty will fall upon Macbeth,
> To which Macduff replies,
> He is already nam'd, and gone to Scone
> To be invested.

Soon after breakfast I set out, crossing on the Forth ferry for threepence, since I had only an eight-horsepower vehicle. Beyond Perth I began looking for Old Scone, a very elusive hamlet. I went backwards and forwards, talked to two housewives, a cauliflower gardener, and a lawn mower (by which I mean a mower of lawns) before I was convinced I had stood on the soil of the ancient Scottish Abbey where Macbeth and other ancient Scottish kings had been crowned. The stone upon which such investitures took place is now enshrined in Westminster Abbey. Hence, I did not actually see the Stone of Scone, settling, instead, for standing where it probably stood. No marker celebrates its history. Old Scone itself is a cluster of about five houses, nasturtium gardens, and a private palace.

Uneasy and insecure as king, Macbeth sought reassurance from the witches. They in turn called up apparitions, one of which told Macbeth that he

...shall never vanquish'd be until
Great Birnam Wood to high Dunsinane Hill
Shall come against him.

So where was Dunsinane Hill? I needed to locate the King's Seat in Dunsinane. That also took more inquiring, for all that remains today is a great chunk of rock in the Sidlaws with a small farm nestled at the bottom and heather growing all around, all around. It is probably a little more than ten miles as the crow flies from the King's Seat to Birnam Wood. Macbeth would have needed powerful binoculars to see Birnam Wood moving. Still I was impressed that I could diagram the action so accurately. And I am the first to admit that knowing all this does not add a whit to the drama of the play that has been packing in audiences for three and a half centuries.

To complete this phase of Shakespeare in Scotland I then drove from Dunsinane Hill to Birnam and spent the night in the Birnam Hotel in the shadow of Birnam Wood. It was a well-appointed hotel with vivid red and blue carpets, brass rods along the stairway, crystal chandeliers, spacious hallways, and huge bathrooms. Twenty-one bouquets of sweet peas, one for every table, decorated the dining room. After dinner I walked up to the soldiers' monument and sat looking out over Dunkeld, the Tay, and Birnam Hill (1,324 feet). Dramatically—not in real life—Macduff's army camouflaged itself with branches cut from the Birnam oaks, giving Macbeth the impression that Birnam Woods was approaching. Suddenly he saw the deception in being told he could not be vanquished until the woods moved to Dunsinane. The caveat must be check witches' forecasts carefully for riddles.

My pursuit of Shakespeare would next take me to the Mop Fair in Stratford-upon-Avon in about two weeks. Therefore, I prepared to leave Edinburgh and make my way leisurely through some Bobby Burns country and on to the Brontes in Yorkshire. When Miss Kenneth, who would give up eating to travel, heard my plans, she begged to go along with me as far as Yorkshire. She even furnished the picnic for the first day's trip.

When we arrived in Ayr that evening, we thought a private home would probably give us some local color as well as information about the area. A policeman recommended "a good one," he said, "right over a superior fish market."

Miss K went in to make inquiries. As she reported to me when she returned to the car, "A woman with a large yellow cat in her arms greeted me. We will have plenty of atmosphere for ten shillings six, the toilet is indoors, and we can wash up in an alcove in the kitchen.

"'In the kitchen?' I said to the woman, 'there in front of all of you?' and she replied, 'We don't mind, really.' So m'thinks, Eve, we will look further for our beds tonight."

Miss K turned out to be an entertaining traveling companion. She probably never would have run out of royal gossip, who had married nobodies, whose marriages were on the rocks, that sort of thing. But lest I tire of gossip, she interspersed it with spicy songs from musicals, and she had the voice to sing them. I still recall the tune but not the words to "I'm One of Cromwell's Ruins."

All was pitch black across the sea when we went for a walk after supper that evening. Lights from an occasional car cast our long, skinny shadows yards ahead of us. A smart wind whipped our faces. "That's a caller breeze," Miss K commented. "Do you know caller?"

"It's a new one to me," I admitted.

"It means fresh, as I have just used it." Then to impress the meaning upon me she burst into song, singing the fishwives' ballad, "Caller Herring." She shared my enthusiasm for all that pertained to Bobby Burns. The following day we visited the Tam o' Shanter Inn, the Old Churchyard, and Brig o'Ayr, and Burns's birthplace in Alloway where we stopped to listen to the curator recite Ingersoll's tribute to Burns for a Swedish visitor. Later he read (though I doubt he needed the book) some of Burns's poems for my tape recorder. His name was Mark Mynn and he was proud of his eighty-three years.

"When did you become so interested in Burns?" Miss K asked him.

"Well, it goes back to when I was a wee lad of seven and refused to eat m'mum's porridge. That evening she set me down beside 'er afore the fireplace and read me a poem by Bobby Burns 'bout appreciating everything God has given us. It just struck me, wee lad that I was, that I liked that Mr. Burns. 'N I've been recitin' 'im to folks now for many a year."

Later, intending to please Miss K's Scottish heart, I said, "Burns seems as universal as Shakespeare."

"Far more universal," she snapped at me. "The common man can understand him."

That night we stayed at the Dunelm Hotel in Durham. It was made up of two buildings, the older built in 1610 and the newer in 1632. Nearly two centuries later in 1801, the newer part became the town house of the Earl of Strathmore. "The Strathmores never did have anything," Miss K muttered. "They were always poor, never went to London, and knew little of society. Why, when the present Queen Mother married George VI (She was a Strathmore) in April, she said she could never face the ordeal of Ascot in June, and when Ascot arrived, she begged off, giving measles as her excuse."

My, my! I knew I was going to miss these little tidbits when Miss K and I parted, but we had one more day together. We went to church in Durham Cathedral the next morning. I found it not a beautiful building inside but frightfully solid. The very long service involved the ordination of five deacons and nine priests by the Lord Bishop of Durham.

After the service I set my sights on Haworth, going by the way of Darlington and Harrogate where I said goodbye to Miss K, giving her kudos for being such a good guide. From Harrogate she would take a bus to a cousin with whom she would spend the next week. As for me I continued to

Shipton, Keighley, and Haworth across beautiful moors and inimitable stone walls, which did not assert themselves until after I left Harrogate. The terrain was rolling and at times steep for Britain. I stopped under an oak tree shortly after leaving Bolton Abbey to eat a cheese and orange snack, the orange first, followed by pure, solid cheese. Cheese and moors. It was a good life. I arrived in Haworth mid afternoon and established a base in the Bronte country for the next month or six weeks.

But before I settled down too seriously with Emily Bronte, I had a date to keep with Mr. Shakespeare. Traditionally the second week of October every year Stratford-upon-Avon celebrates the Mop Fair. Originally the Mop was an occasion for farmers to bring their crops to market and especially for the unemployed to seek employers. It existed long before Shakespeare's day and had grown to something far larger today. The outstanding feature was the roasting of an ox.

Stratford-upon-Avon looked excitingly familiar stretched out before me as I drove in from Welford, down Evesham Place and Church Street and stopped to take my first picture. I had just shot two views of Mason Court when Mr. Holte, my photographer friend, stepped out of his shop. He was just starting for North Wales for the weekend. He told me he had some prize pictures of this year's plays. However, the theater company had allowed him to take them only on the condition he would not sell them. The summer before I had been able to buy half a dozen of his photos from the King Lear production. We agreed to meet for tea after he returns on Tuesday.

King Lear, 1953 Production

The Joneses at the Wayside Inn had a room for me. They were welcoming and proud to show off their new coal grate and lively fire in the lounge. One of the first persons I notified of my presence was Miss Ralston, friend and faithful guide from the previous visit. Because of phlebitis in the spring (you thought I was going to say leg?) she had moved to a downstairs room around the corner at Coniston Guest House.

"Come along," she said when I phoned. "You're exactly what I need this drizzly afternoon." When I arrived she was playing canasta with a youngster whose cold was keeping her home from school. The child, Valerie Ball, maybe fourteen, fifteen years old discussed the plays of the season like an old professor. She likes Barbara Jeffard only as Katherine in the Shrew. Titania is good, but Oberon, no. This Shrew is better than the last. She has seen Romeo and Juliet only twice this season but hopes to see it again before the summer ends.

"I haven't seen Troilus and Cressida. That's for old folks," she informed me.

After tea, I left Miss Ralston, promising to look for her at the play tomorrow night. Forty tickets for each performance at the Shakespeare Memorial Theatre go on sale at ten-thirty the morning of the play. I joined the queue next morning at nine-thirty for Midsummer Night's Dream. The young woman ahead of me said the chap playing Flute that night lives where she does. She told me that in order to learn the Warwickshire accent he had had a ten-year-old read his lines on a tape recorder. Then for days he had played and imitated the tape. She also knew about a minor battle that had broken out backstage last night over some wigs. Such trivia made the hour move swiftly. Soon I was at the window and yes, there was a ticket left for me. During the first interval that evening I sought out Miss Ralston. We indulged in a coffee, discussed the play, and made a date for the next afternoon when I will drive Miss Ralston to her nephew's home in Wilcote.

I dressed for church before breakfast and went straight off after my bacon, egg, toast, and plums, walking on the bowling green side of the river as far as the grain mill and back up past Avonside Hotel to the church, where the vicar preached a metaphorical sermon on gardens and concluded "half a proper gardener's life is spent upon his knees." The day was so beautiful and the sun so warm that after lunch I walked along the Avon again where I watched for a while a boy beside a gypsy caravan playing with a monkey. The river was very busy. The activities included a fishing competition. Every ten feet at a numbered post stood a fisherman with his pole and aspirations. In the meadows were bowls, miniature golf, cricket, and strolling characters.

Folks were arriving by train, car, bus, and bicycle for the Mop Fair, now only two days away. By Monday morning the center of town was completely shut off from vehicle traffic. All day the fair moved into place, the center attraction of which was the whole ox already turning ever so slowly on a spit in the middle of the street in front of the Red Horse Inn. Red coals glowed in what must have been at least an eight-by-four-foot grate. Juices were beginning to drip. Fat was beginning to spit, but portions would not be ready to serve for another twenty-four hours.

Tuesday morning, the day of the fair, I went mid-morning to check on the ox. The crowd had not started to gather around it, and so I was able to take some gruesome, toothsome pictures. After checking out the ox, I headed for the market, where most of the action was taking place. Vendors were still setting up their tents near the ox. Though I had my tape recorder for the mayor's proclamation, I could not resist using a few inches for steer's bellows and pigs' squeaks. I met two women who were waiting for their truck of lambs to come. I finally crawled over the fence into the pen where they were reserving space, the better to pursue our conversation. They assured me that I had not seen anything yet, that every inch of space in the runways would be filled by noon. And while the pens filled, I wandered through the lanes, watching butchers haggling over prices of the early arrivals. For me, the pigs were most interesting of all. In fact, I became so fascinated with them that I did not get back for the mayor's speech after all. When I arrived, chubby little Freddy Baker, the beadle, in his red coat and three-cornered hat, was clanging his bell to clear the way for the mayor's departure on Noah's Ark.

The crowd now swarmed around the ox. It was lunchtime and the beast was ready: rare, medium, or well done. The first slice went for fifty pounds, sterling.

Carving the ox

Hours later the critter was being converted to beef burgers, two shillings a burger. The fixings for the burgers were catered on the sidelines. Except for the ox the Mop was just a mad fair that piled 10,000 people into Bridge and High Street, dancing and eating until midnight. Whether any youth found—or was even looking for—employment as in Shakespeare's day I do not know.

In the six days I was in Stratford I saw four plays in the Shakespeare Memorial Theatre. The Othello was a bit more furious and physical than I had expected with lots of shaking and fury on Anthony Quayle's part. I kept wondering whether his makeup would rub off. Such distractions do not make the best drama. But who am I to question Anthony Quayle? I liked him better as Panderus three nights later in Troilus and Cressida. For my money Romeo and Juliet, on the evening of the Mop, was the best of the four. Zena Walker was convincingly sweet and I wrote in my diary, "Laurence Harvey is earnest." I am not sure forty years later whether that was high praise or not.

I did have tea and some good chatter with Mr. Holte after he returned from his brief holiday in North Wales and tea again with Miss Ralston. The next morning, my bag was packed, my bill was paid, and I was walking the few blocks to where my car was garaged when a car pulled up beside me and a familiar voice said, "Well, how DO you DO?" It was Harry Clark, looking more surprised to see me than I was to see him. It was he who hosted and toasted me the previous summer and saw that I attended the Warwick pageant he was directing. He was dashing into London for the day, but would I have dinner with him that evening.? I explained I was on my way to Yorkshire. "Can't you go tomorrow?" he asked.

"No, I think not," I said. "Next time."

He told me briefly about his own Little Theatre, new since last summer. "The Oliviers will open with Twelfth Night next April 12, and Macbeth is a good possibility for later," he told me. Traffic was backing up behind him and he had to get to the train station, and so we said hasty goodbyes and nice-to-see-yous and went our separate ways.

Miss Ralston had persuaded me to reserve a room in the Coniston Guest House, where she lives, for the Shakespeare Birthday celebration April 22-24. I anticipated I would find more of Shakespeare in the birthday party than I did in the Mop Fair. That is not to say that I did not thoroughly enjoy the Mop. It was not supposed to be about Shakespeare, but rather something he himself doubtlessly experienced many times.

I arrived again in Stratford-upon-Avon on the Thursday before the Birthday Weekend. With a day to spare, I invited Miss Ralston to ride with me to Gloucester. She seemed pleased at the prospect of getting out into the country. Though her arthritis limited her exploring on foot, she was a patient waiter when I strayed and a rich source of history and folklore when we are driving through the countryside. For instance, I picked up a new weather proverb:

If the oak before the ash,
There will be a splash;
If the ash before the oak,
There will be a soak.

In Gloucester I headed for the cathedral, where I poked around, trying to imagine Cromwell's horses and troops bedded down in the nave and transcripts. Some defaced effigies reminded me of his fanatic aversion to things beautiful. I wondered whether that included the beauty in nature, the kind I had seen the past week as I traveled from the Lake District blanketed with daffodils to a friend's home in Brampton where bluetits fed on a lamb's rib hung on a limb outside my bedroom window. Or the sound of a wood pigeon strumming away on his bass viol in a 5:30 A.M. spring concert. But forward with my cathedral prowl: Alderman Blackleich and his wife (1639) reposed undisturbed in elegant grace along the west aisle, as did Sir George Onesiphorus Paul a little farther away from the altar. I climbed 268 steps to the Tower and whispered in the whispering gallery, but neither Cromwell nor King Arthur, who may or may not have ever been buried there, whispered back.

Chargé d'affaires of Laos and wife

On the ride back to Stratford, Miss Ralston sketched some of the things I might look forward to the next two or three days. Diplomats from seventy-four countries would gather for the procession on Saturday. Since one can hardly expect ambassadors, chargé d'affaires, or foreign secretaries in their tall silk hats to be concerned with such details as precedence in the procession, where to find one's flag, what to do with one's wreath or bouquet, or how to unfurl the flag, each delegate has a local steward who is briefed ahead of time, who does the dress rehearsal, so to speak, and meets the dignitary as he or she emerges from the luncheon on Saturday afternoon. I don't know how the local stewards are selected, but through Miss Ralston's intersession, I had become a steward. "A local from the USA," she explained to me, "so that you can be close to things." The dress rehearsal took place that evening, and thanks to Miss Ralston I could not have been closer to the action when the procession started the next afternoon. I was in the midst of it.

Saturday was St. George's Day, St. George and the Dragon and England forever! His flags had been flying from church towers ever since Easter. I had seen them all the way to the lakes and back, even on Rydal Church on the edge of Dora's Field, bobbing with the daffodils. But Stratford-upon-Avon was not giving St. George a nod today, for this was the Bard's three hundred and ninety-first birthday. Mrs. Ball, hostess at the Coniston Guest House, picked a sprig of rosemary from her garden for each of us at breakfast. As Ophelia said,

> There's rosemary, that's for remembrance:
> Pray you, love, remember.

A great bustle stirred throughout Stratford all morning. Diplomats' cars were parked in noticeable, and inconvenient, places, convenient for them, I presume. Storefronts were brightly decorated and the band played in Bancroft Gardens. With rosemary in our lapels, Miss Ralston, Mrs. Cuthbert, Mrs. Wood, and I met for elevensies at the Cobweb on Sheep Street.

The big celebration for the public began as the foreign representatives emerged from their luncheon in the conference hall of the Memorial Theatre. I had known for many years that flags of numerous nations flew for Shakespeare's birthday, but knowing and witnessing are two quite different things. I had been assigned to the chargé d'affaires of Laos. Nepal was ahead of us, Panama ahead of Nepal. Almost miraculously wreath, diplomat, and steward were joined and in place in the Shakespeare Garden. Freddy Baker, the town beadle, gave the signal, and the procession started. It moved through streets two- and three-deep with spectators along Waterside, up Bridge, down High, and along Henley until each notable stood at the foot of the flagpole upon which his country's flag waited, furled. Spaced twenty-five or thirty feet apart, the honoring nations covered much of central Stratford. Holding his memorial wreath, I instructed my chargé d'affaires as to which rope he was to pull when the signal came. It came when the last member of the parade was in place, and at that moment eighty-five flags simultaneously opened to the breezes—the flags of the queen, St. George, the USA, Venezuela, Vietnam, New Zealand, Pakistan, on and on. The crowd cheered. I gasped. I was so excited I almost dropped the Laotian flowers that were in my trust. The idea that one lone man, a saucy, bawdy dramatist, could command such a birthday party three hundred and ninety-one years after his birth almost overcame me.

The beadle heads the procession

After the unfurling, the procession continued on past more sidewalk crowds to Mary Arden's Farm, Shakespeare's birthplace, where the floral offerings were placed. I returned the wreath I had been carrying to the delegate from Laos. The floral tributes were impressive, and I am sure costly. The Chinese, for instance, placed a huge wreath of red carnations. But I was more impressed by the chubby hands of little children clutching two or three daffodils or a bunch of dandelions. After the diplomatic procession passed, any and all spectators (Shakespeare's common men, women, and children) joined the march and laid their own tributes with those from around the world. A wee lassie, maybe four or five years old, with very red cheeks and popping blue eyes, laid her cluster of hyacinths pridefully down atop a bouquet of Canna lilies and snapdragons. Her mum was very proud, too. That evening the Shakespeare Memorial Theatre presented the Oliviers in Twelfth Night.

Children with bouquets

I was fortunate in my British connections. Again Miss Ralston wangled an invitation, this time from the mayor, for me to meet Sunday at the Town Hall and go to church in his procession. Then at the Town Hall she introduced me to Dr. Cogiley, who was an entertaining escort in the procession and at the church. Led, as every procession is, by the bell-bearing, red-coated beadle and escorted by twenty-four policemen (all the part-time policemen they could find uniforms for, Dr. Cogiley told me), a soldier bearing the sword of peace and the mace, the mayor and all his regalia fell into place, followed by the Corporation in black gowns, beaver hats, blue collars and lace ruffs. Next came the birthday dignitaries and last of all the miscellaneous invited guests.

The center section of the church was reserved for those in the procession. The rest of the church was already packed when we arrived. Many of the floral contributions of yesterday covered Shakespeare's grave. Sir Laurence Olivier read the first lesson in his best dramatic diction, and Anthony Quayle, the second. A visiting rector from Cirncester preached the Shakespearean sermon with more literary allusions than I could keep up with.

Back at the Town Hall, guests drank to the health of Queen Elizabeth, to "the immortal memory," the mayor and mayoress, and I had a chance to meet a number of people so that I did not have to stand in a corner and look lost. I met Mr. and Mrs. Shakespeare, who claim relationship to William, and they introduced me to Michael Denison, who played Sir Andrew Aguecheek in Twelfth Night and would be Bertram when All's Well That Ends Well opens Tuesday.

But I would be off to Oxford before Tuesday, by car, even though Dr. Cogiley had confirmed what Harry Clarke once told me that Stratfordians have never taken kindly to motorists on the roads. They would far rather have pedestrians, cyclists, prams, even ambulatory tourists on the streets than motorists. He said they even go so far as to arrest a man for drunken driving who has been drinking and has his car key on his person even though he is in his own home and has no intention of driving. Technically, they reason, he might drive because he has the key.

Love those Stratfordians. They were awfully good to me, as I told Mr. Holte when I went to say goodbye.

Ten years passed before I visited the Bard's hometown again. I was traveling with a group of educators from the States on a program called People-to-People. It was the brainchild of President Eisenhower, a project to bring together people of like interests in different countries. Our group of twenty visited schools and universities in Dublin, what was then Leningrad, Moscow, Oxford, Geneva, and Paris. While in Oxford, we took a day's outing to visit Stratford-upon-Avon. Not wanting the usual tourists' tour, I took the day to visit some special haunts and friends. Shortly after lunch I went to Mr. Holte's photography shop. We had not kept in touch since my last visit, and I was dismayed to find a woman in his place at the counter.

"I am looking for Mr. Holte," I explained.

"Oh, Mr. Holte retired three years ago," she said, then seeing my disappointment, added, "but he lives upstairs. I am his daughter."

I explained how and when I knew him, and she felt sure he would want to see me. I waited while she went for him.

"Mr. Holte," I exclaimed when he appeared, "why has a young man like you retired?"

"It might be because I have such a competent daughter to run the shop." Then he added, "I can't recall your name, but I know you. You took the picture of Salisbury Cathedral with the spire in the corner. I had never seen that before, and I've never forgotten it."

When I explained I was in Stratford only for the day, he immediately said, "Then you must go with me to my little cottage on the river for tea."

"Sounds good to me," I said. So off he went, first upstairs to change his slippers and then around the corner to fetch his car. We drove maybe five or six miles along the Avon before he pulled in beside a little two-room building perched on the edge on the riverbank. The kitchen corner of the living room was fully equipped for making tea, but first he brought two chairs outside where we could talk and watch the Avon flow by.

"I tell folks I come down here fishing," he chortled, "but I spend more of my time daydreaming, reading, watching the butterflies. I love it down here."

We talked for a couple of hours about what we had each been doing, about the plays at the theatre, about the joys of retirement. I noted that he had Canada geese instead of mute swans swimming in his river. And why are they called Canada geese in England? Then it was time for tea. He made the tea and "played mother," but when we finished, he said, "You will find the tea towels in the top drawer and I bet you are good at washing up." So I cleaned up the kitchen and tried to leave it as tidy as I found it. Then it was time for me to leave. Once back in Stratford, Mr. Holte and I parted, and I went looking for my group.

Fifteen or more years elapsed before I saw Stratford-upon-Avon again. I was visiting with a friend who had never been to Great Britain. In a rented car we made our way to the home of the Bard. But what a culture shock awaited me. If I had never known before, I would have now understood what the Japanese philosopher Hyakawa meant by, "You cannot step into the same river twice." The Stratford that abhorred motorcars in my day was now a turmoil of traffic. Round-abouts, one-way traffic, car parks abounded. I could scarcely find the Avon and the theater, which had been so walkable formerly. I did not find a parking place and drove on through the town, explaining this was not the Stratford I knew. Doubtlessly Shakespeare still stands in Bancroft Garden and today's best actors and actresses perform Hamlet and Macbeth in the Memorial Theatre, but memories must suffice for me.

Cheltenham Literature Festival

(diary excerpt)
Cheltenham
October 5 and 6, 1954

On my way to the Cheltenham Literature Festival I stopped briefly in Ludlow, attracted by the Feathers Hotel, a stunning black and white timbered structure of the sixteenth century. It is one of the first eight licensed houses in Great Britain, getting its license during the reign of Henry VII, having been a private house before that. Part museum, it contains relics of Henry VIII, Elizabeth I, James I, and William III. This morning it was exuding a tantalizing aroma of freshly baked bread that seemed to waft throughout the village. As I wandered back to the car park, the Buttercross clock struck twelve. After the twelfth bell, the chimes went on to play "Bluebells of Scotland." "...and it's oh in my heart that I love da, da, da, da." Maybe the words will come to me tomorrow.

Arriving in Cheltenham, I went first to the Information Bureau for a program of the literature festival the town is hosting this weekend. The woman at the desk offered to phone the Overton Lodge Hotel and reserve a room for me for two nights. I had just time to run up and claim it before hiking back to the town hall, where I was happy to find I could get tickets for all the festival performances, including the mayor's luncheon tomorrow.

With all that accomplished, I was still in time for the first lecture of the day, History and Literature, presented by A. L. Rouse, Elizabethan historian and Oxford don pinch hitting for Margaret Irwin. The substitution pleased me to no end, since I became familiar with Rouse recently while completing my master's thesis at Columbia. Not knowing Margaret Irwin, I couldn't know what I was missing.

It was pouring (a popular British activity I have come to accept) when I finished looking over the book displays outside the lecture hall, and so I ducked into the nearest restaurant, Tiffan's Snack Bar, for a cup of soup and then drizzled back to the town hall to await the evening lecture by Christopher Fry, whose work I have long admired. It was a rather shy Fry but poetically and metaphorically very satisfying. I could even go so far as to say delightful. I tried not to let my mouth hang open.

The next day at the mayor's luncheon at the Queen's Hotel, I found myself somewhere between the agneau and the sorbet au Kirsch composing an ode to be titled "Puligny-Montrachey among the Carnations" when a dark-eyed lady across the table from me leaned into the Carnations and inquired, "I have a feeling you are a stranger among strangers. Are you an American?"

"That I am," I acknowledged.

"You are having a good time, aren't you ?" So "Puligny-Montrachey, etc.,…" is lost to the world. The conversation that followed made up for the loss.

The young man to my right soon joined in. He was from Slimbridge,[1] he told me, a small town between Gloucester and Bristol. It has the distinction of being the home of Peter Scott, bird artist. As we talked, we were periodically interrupted by the toastmaster with, "Your Worship, my lords, ladies, and gentlemen, pray silence for a toast to the queen" or "Pray silence for Lord Russell."

My young informant was bouncing with enthusiasm for Lord Russell, our luncheon speaker. Being a foreigner, I could be excused—maybe—for not knowing his book, Scourge of the Swastika, had necessitated his stepping down from a high judicial position. The book has sold 56,000 copies in its first six weeks of publication (so perhaps I should have known) and he has received over six hundred congratulatory letters, plus a visit from a rucksacked Tennesseean who arrived at his home by taxi. He told this story himself. After about fifteen minutes of talking about nothing, the visitor drawled embarrassedly, "I've come, Lord Russell, to congratulate you on your eightieth birthday." Whereupon Lord Russell, who is scarcely pushing sixty, explained that he was not the revered Sir Bertram Russell.

The nucleus of Lord Russell's address to us was the importance of keeping Germany in its place now the war is over. He also lamented the state Great Britain has reached that it cannot accept a recently published song about Anthony titled "Always the Bridemaid but Never the Bride." When humor is lost, what is left?

André Maurois, another author I was excited to hear and see in person, shared the head table with Lord Russell and spoke briefly on "Freedom in Writing." Next we adjourned to a flower-bedecked stage and auditorium full of boarding school girls waiting to hear Nevil Coghill's address, "Shakespeare's Tragedies."

The festival concluded in the evening with a rousing debate between a quiet, unassuming man from Oxford and an Oscar Wildish don from Cambridge, Resolved: The backbone of the novel is the plot. Cambridge, arguing for the negative, won limpidly, but devastatingly.

The Brontes

THE LORRY PLUNGING down the cobblestoned street swerved onto the pavement, its only acknowledgment of my Morris Minor straining up the hill. Past dark, stone shops I drove, past shops joined like little children holding hands, past the Bronte Bakery on the left, past the Bronte Antique Shop on my right. Through an arched passage to the right flashed a view of undulating fields. So this was Haworth, a small dark dot midst miles of grassy moors.

At the top of the hill the road jogged to the left. Dead in front of me stood the Bronte Guest House, another dark, stone building, this one brightened by window boxes of red geraniums. Parking on the tiny flagstone triangle at the entry, I sat a moment, fizzy with anticipation of what adventures awaited me in this strange new world. It was September. The grain was being harvested. The heather was in bloom.

Inside, Kathleen greeted me cordially. Yes, a room was available for a month. Six weeks? As long as I wanted. She led me up bright red-and-blue carpeted stairs to a modest room looking out upon fields of grain enclosed by stone walls. Beyond, the moors were dotted with sheep. George would fetch my bags.

"Wat bringsya t'Haworth?" Kathleen asked, her Yorkshire accent strange to my ear.

"I'm visiting and photographing places my students read about in English literature," I told her.

"N hud b'gavenya tha'prity geeft?" she asked in lilting, clipped phrases.

I explained the Ford Fellowship for which my school board had given me a year's leave of absence.

After a few more exchanges, which were like speaking in two languages, she departed, saying, "Mineyacomb d'nfertea 'tfow."

From the bedroom window I looked across the town below, a jigsaw puzzle of gray roofs and chimney pots. I could see why Haworth is called "the grim north" in contrast to the softer, thatch-roofed villages of Dorset and

I parked on the flagstone triangle

Devon. Through the years, smoke from local industries has blackened the locally quarried stone from which all buildings in Haworth are built. The "dry stane dykes," which line roads and divide grain field from grain field, are equally dingy gray. The fenced-in fields reminded me of Robert Frost's "Mending Walls":

> He's all pine and I am apple orchard.
> My apples will never get across
> And eat the cones under the pines, I tell him...

When I went down for tea at four, I met George and Sybil Standish, who own and run the guest house. George had already fetched my bag from the car. Kathleen, Mrs. Standish explained, was their daughter, on holiday from Bristol for a few days. I also met Pincher, a tea-drinking sheepdog and would-be host. Other guests would join us shortly, Mrs. Standish thought. They were walking on the moors.

Dry stane dykes divide the fields

I had just taken another ginger biscuit and was going to ask about the portrait over the fireplace when a new face appeared at the door.

"Comb in," Sybil said, "en meet our new guest. From America."

Mrs. Shuttleworth had stopped for a moment on her way home from the bakery, where she had gone to purchase oatcakes for her own tea.

"Comb and sit down," Sybil urged. "Tak a breath."

"Thot hill! Geets steeper evra week." Mrs. Shuttleworth sighed. Then turning to me, she stated more than asked, "Yoof comb ta'see the Brontes."

I acknowledged I had. "N yood bay goin' first to Upper Withins?"

"Upper Withins?" I hesitated.

"Guests allyus goo t' Upper Withins. They cull't Wuthering Heights, Emily Bronte's Wuthering Heights."

"It's still standing, I understand."

"Oh, bot barley," she agreed.

Over another ginger biscuit and a second cup of tea, Mrs. Shuttleworth told me about Upper Withins. Roddie was the last man to live there. She remembered him. He came there after the First World War. Had been a soldier. Had a few sheep, some chickens. He ran a little craft shop just below the Bronte Guest House and did some shining and polishing for the antique dealer next door.

"You knew him, then," I said.

"Ah, ye. He wuz on'f us. But he left Upper Withins twelve, fifteen years ago. 'Twuz toomblin doon. Just died the pahst year [1953]."

She told me, too, about Percy Smith, a local artist who was sketching Wuthering Heights one day when he heard strange human cries coming from the dilapidated farm house. When he went to investigate, he found a man tied to a chair. Before he could decide what he should do, he saw Roddie coming home from Stanbury. "Oh, yes," said Roddie. "that's m'brother from the asylum. I allus tie 'im oop when I go t'town."

"Bot I mus' be on m'way now," Mrs. Shuttleworth concluded. "Mr. Shuttleworth will be wantin' 'is tea."

"You live nearby?" I asked.

"Jus' doon the lane. You mus' comb to tea soon." And off she went with her oatcakes.

The next morning I set out on foot for Upper Withins, walking across Parson's Field to the edge of town where a moorland path turns off to the right. After a mile or so I came to the Bronte Waterfalls, which that day were a bare trickle seeping twenty or thirty feet from the quarries above, scarcely the rush of water Charlotte Bronte described a century earlier when she wrote

> I had often wished to see it [the waterfalls] in its winter power, so we [she and her husband] walked on. It was fine indeed, a perfect torrent racing over the rocks, white and beautiful.

I lingered, picturing the Bronte children, those little tykes, coming all this way to play. They would have crossed the field beyond the parsonage, where their widowed father churned out his sermons of hell and damnation, and followed the same path I had through the bracken.

To walk in the footsteps of the Brontes is to populate the moors with scenes from their novels. The water trickling from waterfalls runs into Sladen Beck just beyond where I was standing that morning. A few precariously placed stones bridged the stream. Maybe this was where Nelly, taking a shortcut from Wuthering Heights to town, got her feet wet and caught the cold that kept her in bed during the crucial weeks Cathy was visiting Linton Heathcliffe. From this spot Emily, as a child, could have seen, as I did that morning, Upper Withins silhouetted against the sky and imagined her Wuthering Heights.

I crossed Sladen Beck on the teetery stones and picked my way past bogs and through the heather to a path that led to the Heights. The gradual climb continued until at the end I stood in the shadow of that tumbled down building. Looking back across the waves of moors under a cloudless sky, I thought of Emily's lines in "A Farewell to Alexandria":

I've seen the dell in July's shine
As lovely as an angel's dream,
Above, heaven's depth of blue divine,
Around, the evening's golden beam.

I've seen the purple heather-bell
Look out by many a storm-worn stone:
And oh, I've seen such music swell'
Such wild notes wake these passes lone.

And they are lone.

Pincher was a frequent companion on my jaunts over the moors. He pretended to be a guide but secretly longed for an opportunity to chase sheep, for he was both by breed and temperament a sheepdog. "What do you say?" I asked him the morning I set out for Ponden Hall, the model for Emily's Thrushcross Grange. "Want t' come?" He woofed in the dialect of a North Country dog his willingness to join me.

"Ya nedna kip'm on's cheen lesya overtike soom shape," George said. "Mind 'e locks t'roundoop shape."

Off Pincher and I went, following the road to Stanbury. Two miles along our way, I recognized Ponden Hall, or the Grange, off to my left, but I could not see a public access from the road. Puzzled, I stopped at a little house to ask whether I might follow the path behind it to the Grange. It was the oddest little house I had ever seen, what appeared to be a single room atop a single room. As I approached, an elderly woman with one front tooth came to meet me. Her rheumatiz, she said, slowed her up these days. But nothing slowed her tongue.

"Thiz's owd Timmy's 'ouse," she greeted me. "Yav hard of'm?"

"He was a weaver?" I asked, for I could hardly deny having heard of "old Timmy," the last of the home handloom weavers.

"Ay, 'n fine fooak in thar carriage bin a purpose t'see 'm. Thay'dleeaf an odder feer soom cotton…three, fow, twelve yards. Suntime twenty. 'Im cuna weave fas enif. 'Im cudna fit op." She rattled on. Her lower jaw with its single tooth just to the right of center worked up and down like a treadle. His loom, she told me, was in the upper room. Visitors came from miles to leave orders and watch him work. "'E dinna know exactly 'is birthdate. But 'e war owd. Curly whiskers allo'er ims faaece."

"You knew him?" I asked.

"Me, Mottie? Alorda, E'did."

When I made bold to ask how old she was, she appeared to ignore my question, and so I moved on to the purpose of my stopping. "Will anyone object to my walking through here? I want to visit Ponden Hall."

"Nobbut live there," she replied. "Mr. Dyson, 'e belongs Ponden Hall."

"Where does he live?"

"Jus yon. See thot cheemly pot risin' behind the dykes? Thot be 'is. E'll gif t'key t'ya if ya but ask."

Having thanked Mattie, I walked on to the house she had pointed out. Mr. Dyson had gone to Colne for the day and taken the key with him. I was welcome, though, his wife said, to look around the property.

I returned to "owd Timmy's" house to follow the path. As I turned into the track, Mattie came out again. I told her Mr. Dyson was out of town. Without responding to that bit of information, she said, "Fur 's E kin reckon, E'm eighty-six."

Ponden Hall evoked images of Mr. Lockwood, the new tenant in the opening chapters of Wuthering Heights and Edgar and Isabelle, who later lived there. I photographed the kitchen garden wall, the stanchioned windows that kept Heathecliff at bay, the horse steps from which hoop-skirted women entered carriages, and the Grange itself set amidst acres of brown bracken. I would return another day for pictures of the interior—the stone floors, large beams, and decorative rosettes in the ceiling, all of which I could vaguely discern, gazing through the windows, but which appeared to be much as Emily describes them.

It was afternoon when Pincher and I reached the road again. We shared bread and marmalade salvaged from breakfast and headed back to the village, this time following the moorland paths.

• • •

In the following weeks my life played itself out in two theaters—the moors and the lounge. As was the British custom, guests withdrew after dinner to the lounge for café au lait. One evening early in my visit four of us sat silently before the coal-burning fireplace, sipping demi-tasses and pursuing our varied interests. Mr. Pruitt, local choirmaster and permanent resident, sat at a table across the room from me, absorbed in some sheets of music. I say he was absorbed, as he might have said I was absorbed in reading Vilette. Actually I was surreptitiously watching him twitch. He had a nervous tic, which I first mistakenly attributed to self-consciousness, for he was a very shy man. There he sat, scratching music notes and twitching. He added, I thought, a bit of British atmosphere. A character from Dickens perhaps? Yes, that was it—Uriah Heep.

Miss Eliott, formerly of South Africa and now a nurse somewhere in Yorkshire, was spending a fortnight researching the Brontes. That evening she was comparing two biographies, balancing Margaret Lane on one knee and Mrs. Gaskell on the other. She was particularly interested in real places that might have suggested various sites in Wuthering Heights. This evening she had chosen the chair closest to the fire in the grate. One reason for lingering

Ponden Hall (horse steps lower left)

in the lounge after the coffee is finished is that Yorkshire bedrooms are not heated.

Why need they be when those wonderful aluminum or ceramic hot water bottles will find their way into guests' beds each night around ten o'clock? When autumn puts a nip in the air, the fire in the grate tempts guests to linger.

The fourth guest on this particular evening was Sarah Benham, who was trying to finish the book she had borrowed from the collection on the mantel, the mantel over which Charlotte Bronte's portrait looked benignly down upon us. Her holiday was over. She had to return to Southport the next afternoon. Sybil disclaimed any responsibility for the confusion among the books. "Guests take some and leave others," she explained, "a kind of round robin library." Some standard Brontes were there—Gaskell, Lane, Halliwell Sutcliffe's Men of the Moors, side by side with Why Waterloo? and Travels in East Anglia. Two collections of Longfellow's poetry nestled among other miscellany.

Sybil once asked a Japanese guest what British writers are translated into Japanese. The first to come to mind was Bobby Burns. Fancy this in Japanese:

> Wee, sleekit, cowrin', tim'rous beastie,
> O, what a panic's in thy breastie!
> Thou needa start awa sae hasty,
> Wi' bickering brattle!
> I wad be laith to rin an' chase thee,
> Wi' murd'rous pattle!

Sybil appeared just before ten o'clock with tea and ginger biscuits. Suddenly, like a triggered Ouija board, the room came to life. Conversation roamed from generalities to particulars of European travel, passport and visa horror stories and finally to SybIl's telling us how very amusing American tourists can be. To make her point she regaled us with the didos of three young American women who spent a week in Haworth the past summer.

The fire in the grate burned low before Mr. Pruitt shuffled his music sheets and muttered, "Gooid neet." Sarah, Miss Eliott, and I soon followed. As Pepys would say, "And so to bed."

Early in my visit the dining room was as quiet as the lounge. Miss Eliott and I might exchange in soft tones a few details of our day as we made our way to our separate tables. Mr. Pruett was too shy to be brought into any conversation, though I had tried unsuccessfully to find a common interest. Therefore the click of soupspoons usually exceeded the volume of the human voice as we set about our dinner. One evening I was alone in the dining room, neither Miss Eliott nor Mr. Pruett having shown up. I was just finishing my dessert of fried bananas and apricots when Miss Eliott appeared, a bit frazzled for such a dignified person. She had been wandering about Oldfield and Oakworth. Thinking it too late to stick to the footpaths, she had started straight across the fields. When she came to a stream too wide to jump, she had taken off her shoes and stockings and waded across. With her British reserve and my natural reticence shattered, I invited her to join me at my table and tell me about her day. She was still concerned about the directions in Wuthering Heights, somehow feeling one should be able to pinpoint on an ordnance map every place mentioned in Emily's fiction. That evening she wanted to move Wuthering Heights to Keighley moor. Earlier she had wanted to move Gimmerton to Oakworth. I was sorry her holiday was nearly over. We might have shared more Bronte lore, but she would be leaving Haworth at the end of the week.

The moors in heather

Sybil said Wycollar Hall was seven miles by road, but if I climbed a five-bar gate two miles beyond Ponden Hall and walked through the fields I would save a mile. Wycollar was Charlotte's Ferndeane Manor in Jane Eyre. Pincher and I found the five-bar gate. I climbed over; he scooted under and soon found himself on his chain as we walked among a flock of sheep. I was beginning to wonder whether I had scaled the wrong gate when, walking through a pasture of cows, I spotted a large stone house in the distance. Despite the distance, the huge letters T E A S across the south side of the building stood out prominently. Soon only a stile stood between Parson Lee Farm and me.

A round-faced, rosy-cheeked woman came to the door. She assured me that another short mile would bring me to Wycollar Hall. "Boot mindya, luv," she cautioned, "t'Hall's joost ruins." She would be glad to get lunch for Pincher and me...anything we wanted. I suggested a small salad and tea. She boiled an egg, fresh from the hen yard, she told me, and added tomatoes, grated cheese and lettuce with white bread, raisin bread, brown bread, tea and cakes. Pincher was welcome to share with me. And did, drinking tea from a saucer on the floor.

Lunch over, my hostess presented me with the tab neatly lettered on a piece of cereal box. It read "Mrs. Wilson, one tea, one shilling." But she did not have change for my ten-shilling note. "Thot's a'right, luv. You'll comb

Through fields joined by stiles.

book someday." She wished us well, and we set out once more for Wycollar Hall, which was, indeed, only rubble. Rubble...and memories of Rochester, coat flying, as he dashed toward Ferndeane Manor. Someone sat at an easel sketching the ruins in the afternoon sunshine. A brook ran nearby with two footbridges. It was a Kodak moment.

I walked on through Wycollar hamlet before turning right onto a footpath that took me straight up through three fields joined by stiles to the main road. I stopped once to ask a farmer whether I was going right and hoping to glean some information about Wycollar Hall. He was, however, far more interested in crops and the rain supply in the United States than in Wycollar ruins. Walking on, I encountered a sow with a dozen piglets wallowing in a pool of mud, and at the bottom of the next stile landed in mud myself. "...glorious, glorious mud; there's nothing quite like it for cooling the blood," sang the hippo. Once on the high road, I could have reached the guesthouse in a couple of hours, but Pincher and I were happy to accept a ride before we had walked a mile. A month later I returned to Parson Lee Farm with Nancy Fisher, an American staying at the guesthouse. This time driving to Wycollar Hall and walking "the short mile" to lunch and the settlement of my earlier debt.

I found a second home with the Shuttleworths where I was always welcome for tea...or even supper on several occasions. We pored over pictures Mr. Shuttleworth, a retired photographer, had taken years ago. I never tired of listening to him reminisce. One evening he and his brother were talking in the kitchen as I sat with Mrs. S in the next room. "Listen t'em," she said during a pause in our conversation. I listened, trying to catch the drift. "Ya donna wat thy're sayin', d'ya?"

I agreed that I didn't.

"Thay'r talkin' thar boyhood dialect, the real Yorkshire language. E m'self fond it 'ard t'folla. A bloke from Devonshire or Warwickshire or Sussex conna follow." I thought of Joseph in Wuthering Heights and Emily's attempt to express his speech in old Yorkshire dialect. Mr. Shuttleworth agreed if I brought my tape recorder along some evening, he would read Joseph's conversation in both the dialect and the translation. They introduced me to a program on the wireless called the Northcountryman, a local color program.

Mr. S gave me several photographs he had taken years before of places associated with the Brontes and a couple of books, saying he had no further use for them. One, I especially treasured, A Spring-time Saunter: Round and About Bronte-land. He told me tales of local characters no longer with us, like Tom Stell, a friend of his father. "Ya walk oop Snowden Lane, cross the quarries 'comb bak byin the Hilltop Café you'll foind Tom Stell's Seat." Tom used to climb up to that spot on the moors and say, "This be a gradley [beautiful] spot." Friends erected the memorial seat, quarried in one piece on the local moor, in 1932. I made the walk to Tom Stell's seat one "gradley" day. Sun rays beamed through scudding clouds, streaming down on distant moors, and the wind said lovely things.

The Shuttleworths were also generous guides. We were a threesome. I had the car; Mr. S had the knowledge; and Mrs. S often had the picnic. Once Mr. S offered to go with me to Stone Gappe the next day if the weather were promising. When I stopped the next morning to ask whether they considered the day "promising," Mrs. S was already preparing the picnic. "Zoots na gradley but gud fer this teema year," Mr. S said.

On our way to Stone Gappe, we stopped to admire a favorite view. Mr. Shuttleworth recalled days during the war when he stood at that site spotting aircraft. Though ten years had elapsed since the end of World War II, tales of it came readily to mind. Folks used to give him a ham or a dozen eggs or a pound of butter—all stringently rationed commodities. A policeman stopped him once. He wanted a ride and unsuspectingly crawled in beside a smuggled ham. "He neeva guessed," Mr. S said, chuckling, "but E was happy when he thonked me fer 'is ride and went 'is way."

Days in Haworth were by no means always "gradley." "This is a museum day if I ever saw one," I mused to myself as I ate my porridge one morning. I even communicated the thought to Mr. Pruett at the table next to me. "Yes," he replied, blinking and keeping his eyes on the porridge rapidly receding from his bowl. Rain pelted the cobblestones outside the open door in the hall. The Standishes left all outside doors open wide even though brown leaves and rain blew through the hallway. Upstairs a line of clothes I had washed six days before and strung between the washbasin and bedstead was not yet dry. My suede shoes seemed as wet as when I was caught in a shower two days before. I thought of the many people in Yorkshire novels who get soaking wet, catch cold, and expire or spend the winter in bed.

Yes, I would spend the day in the Parsonage Museum. Wind slashed the trees when I crossed the street. Rain beat against my mac as I made my way up the lane past the churchyard. Wet, brown leaves clung to the flat, gray gravestones. Once inside, I settled down to read Transactions, the yearbooks of the Bronte Society. They contain articles by members and reports of annual meetings.

Shortly after noon three bus loads of girls from Hull Teacher Training School arrived at the museum, each wrapped 'round and 'round in her long tri-colored scarf of orange, blue, and black, the school colors. By that time I was reading playbills and prospectuses. As the clatter of the girls increased, I left to seek some quiet in the church. A few girls had also found their way there as had one lone Japanese lad, who had come to Haworth, he said, to pay "homage to this captivating family." He was searching for the Bronte memorial on the west wall. Together we found it as well as the plaque in the south aisle.

The rain had let up slightly before I returned to the guesthouse for tea. George met me in the hall and said, "We have another guest tonight." He shook his head in amusement as he continued. "He's a maverick from London. Pops up 'ere without warnin' two er three teems a year. Niver brings a bag. Joost arrives. This afternoon a shower caught 'im. Come in soakin' wet 'n no dry clothes. Is upstairs now tryin' t'git into one of m'suits. You'll meet 'im at dinner."

And so I did. What a contrast to Mr. Pruett. He was not loquacious, but comfortably talkative. Not the least apologetic to be squeezed into George's suit two sizes too small for him. When he entered the dining room, George introduced him as Mr. Phelps. But with merely a "May I?" Mr. Phelps moved his place setting to my table and held my chair for me saying, "Call me Kenneth."

"Been here before?" he asked as George placed the soup du jour before us. The "du jour" was liver that evening.

"First visit," I told him.

"Where've you been?" I enumerated my many visits around the area, and for each one he had an anecdote or jot of information new to me.

"Have you been to Brussels? Where Emily once went to teach?"

"And was so homesick? No...no, I'm just beginning my Bronte odyssey."

"Come with me sometime. I keep going back. Of course, she couldn't have borne it. Far too sensitive. Have you read the rubbish about her mysterious lost love? The whole debate has arisen over a careless misreading of her poem 'Farewell to Alexandria.' Simple as that. There was no 'lost love.' Come to London. I'll show you the poem in her own handwriting...and all those tiny books the children wrote. They're all in the British Museum. I'll show you. You comin' to London soon?"

I really didn't need to talk. Just listen. He was bursting with information about the Brontes. Then to my surprise he said as we continued our discussion in the lounge over café au lait that Thomas Hardy was his first love. He proceeded to quote poems of Hardy, some in snatches and others in their entirety. Belatedly, I asked, "Are you a teacher?"

"Uh-uh."

"Then you must be an actor."

"Heavens, no. I work in an office, a very dull office doing very dull things in the name of Her Majesty. But I have my dreams. In my youth," he confessed, smiling, "I wrote poetry under the influence of Hardy. Even took some to the second Mrs. Hardy for her appraisal."

"What did she say?"

"Said it was much, and I quote, 'in the Hardy style but not original enough for publication.'"

"And then?"

"I grew up. Well, she was right. I never submitted anything. Do you know that Hardy came once to Haworth?"

"No, I've never heard that."

"He did. He visited the Parsonage and discussed with Mr. Mitchell [the curator] similarities between Cathy and Tess."

"How do you know all these things?" I asked.

"Dunno, just read a lot, talk with people, ask questions. The Brontes have a grip on me. Sometimes I just haf't jump a train 'n get up 'ere...walk the moors, think. Will you walk with me in the morning?"

"Maybe, probably. Sure I will."

The rain was soft, not pelting, when we started out with Pincher late the next morning. George insisted Kenneth borrow his mac. I had my own raincoat, well used after three weeks in Haworth. We walked as far as Harbor Lodge, the gamekeeper's house, but a motorbike scramble near the quarries thwarted our efforts to experience the loneliness Emily's poems and novel describe. Pincher, who had started out not on a leash, ended up tied to Kenneth's red scarf. Rain clouds were gathering when we turned and started back to the guesthouse.

We were still on the footpath when the heavens opened and a shower engulfed us. The wind blew with such force that the collar of my mac, whipping hard and fast, stung my face. We stood, back to the wind, until the shower passed, Pincher crouching at our feet. As the rain slackened, the irrepressible Kenneth, addressing the freshened bogs, quoted:

I battled against the wind today
In a lonely, moorland place;
Angrily over the hills it drove
Arrows of rain into my face:

Like a scourage of grace.

Savage and stern were the moors today;
And my fight was nearly vain;
Only the whip o' the wind in my face
And the stinging steel of the rain.
But I'll go again.

"'...and the stinging steel...' Don't you love it? Don't you feel that's exactly right?" he asked.

"Exactly," I agreed, "and I've just experienced 'the whip of the wind.'"

"Remarkable woman, that Emily," he said, more to himself than to me as we resumed our walk.

A little farther on he suddenly turned and faced me. "Do I remind you of Heathcliffe?" he asked.

"Hadn't thought of it."

"Well, think of it. I'd like to play Heathcliffe in a film. I think I could manage it."

He left after Sunday dinner to catch the train in Keighley, saying again that he wanted to show me the Bronte manuscripts in the British Museum. "When are you coming to London?" he asked, not for the first time.

"Oh, not for a long time."

"How long?"

"At least a couple of months."

"Set a date. Set a date and time, and I will meet you on the steps of the British Museum."

"Okay, the eighteenth of January at 12 noon."

"I'll be there. On the eighteenth step," and off he went. I never expected to see him again, maverick that he was. However, should he turn up, what better way to spend my birthday.

When Sybil Standish went into hospital for surgery in mid-October, her sister and brother-in-law, the MacIntyres, came from Argyll to help George, and with their arrival came an end to silent evenings in the lounge. Oh, we had our café au lait, as usual, but Mr. MacIntyre was a gregarious chap and a true-blue Scottish story teller. I heard tales of their freighter trip to what Mrs. MacIntyre called "higgledy-piggledy" Canada and of their married life just after World War I when they cooked in one sauce pan for a year and paid three pound a week for board and room while he was earning two pound eighteen. We heard tales of Inverary, Mr. Mac's boyhood home. He took his bride to visit there one blizzardy night shortly after they married. His friend Sandy Gillis drove twenty-six miles to meet them at the station. Then they had to drive with the top down to keep from blowing off the road. I thought he might have taken a little poetic license with that one until a few weeks later I saw a headline in the Morning Post: GALE BLOWS LORRIES OFF MOUNTAIN ROAD. Hundred-mile-an-hour gusts had lifted and hurled about a dozen lorries over the side of the mountain road, called Rest and Be Thankful Hill, in Argyll, not many miles from Inverary.

Mac told no end of stories of ghosties and ghoulies and things that go bump in the night, of a missing hired girl who was found a month later under a crag, "starch still stiff in her apron," of milk sent to a lab for inspection where it arrived with the container empty. Mysterious.

He was surprised I had not yet visited the Black Bull. A must, he said, for anyone seriously interested in the Brontes. And I agreed. So off we went Saturday night to the pub across the street, fifty feet from the guesthouse, going first to what was still called Branwell's room. A window looked out across the graveyard to the parsonage, a window to which Emily would sometimes run to warn her brother that papa was storming down the lane to fetch him. Branwell would escape through the window and be lounging languidly in the parlor at home when Father returned.

Mac had me sit in Branwell's chair and tug the pull rope for service. Service, however, was no longer available in that room. We moved on to the bar, where Mr. Mac ordered light ale for me and introduced me to the couple sitting next to us. The husband had been a policeman but was more recently a gamekeeper. As I nursed my ale, I talked with him about gamekeeping and learned that the black and white bird I have been seeing on my walks, with a prominent tuft on the back of its neck, is a lapwing, also called a plover or pee wit.

Mr. Toothill, who had joined our group as we talked, was an engineer and also a singer on the BBC. At his suggestion we moved into the singing room where Molly of the Ducking Well was singing "The Sunshine of Your Smile." Later, Mr. Toothill "for the benefit of our American guest" led the group in the ballad "On Ilkley Moor Baht Hot[Without Hat]." Before the ballad was finished a Salvation Army couple came into the room, looked around, and decided to join in the singing. The ballad finished, they moved among us with their kettles, collecting sixpence and shillings to help the needy and distressed. The evening was so wonderfully companionable we remained until the closing call, "'Tis toime! 'Tis toime!"

I woke the next morning to the patter of rain outside my window, the seventh or eighth day (I had lost track) of almost continuous rain. After breakfast, I donned my raincoat, pulled on my rain hat, and walked across the street, past the site of the previous night's adventure to the church. We didn't sing:

> Praise Him that He gave the rain
> To mature the ripening grain...

But Mr. Dickson, the rector, did pray that "this endless rain may cease so that the harvest may be gathered." At three that afternoon every rain cloud suddenly vanished. All was blue sky. Barbara, a weekend guest from London who described herself as a milk maid and who had been in the land army during the war, dashed out for a walk. Pincher and I soon followed. But by five o'clock it was raining again. In all fairness to the power of prayer, I must admit that Monday dawned bright and blue-skied. I didn't see another drop of rain for nearly forty-eight hours. Whether farmers finished gathering their grain in that time, I couldn't say.

I had been in Haworth nearly five weeks. I had visited most of the places associated with the Brontes' lives or novels, even driving to Cowan Bridge where the two little sisters had gone briefly to boarding school. I had yet to visit Anne's grave in Scarborough. Nor had I been to High Sunderland Hall or Law Hill, two places connected with Emily's aborted effort to teach school. Several folks had assured me nothing existed any longer at High Sunderland Hall, that the last parts were torn down nearly two years ago. I knew, though, that parts of it were inhabited as recently as eight years ago when Ernest Raymond wrote In the Steps of the Brontes. Further, I found it marked on my ordnance map. I had to see for myself.

The debris that lay scattered around the site of what once was High Sunderland Hall seemed more suitable for an archeologist than a pursuer of English literature. I spent more than an hour pawing through the rubble, hoping to find something I could attach some significance to, but to no avail. Chunks of carved stone or a slab of what was probably once part of a fireplace conveyed nothing of Emily and her frustrations in her attempt to teach school. A section of new stone wall was already starting to claim High Sunderland Hall. I soon abandoned the site and drove back two miles to Law Hill, where Emily boarded through the week.

I knocked on the door and asked whether I might look about the property and take some pictures. "Sure e'nuf, love," a friendly woman greeted me, "but step in 'n'ave a cuppa tea first, love." I explained my interest in Emily Bronte. She was Mrs. Ben Marshall, she said. I asked about the warehouse next door.

"Now Daddy kin tell ya more 'bout things than I kin," she said and as though on cue out of nowhere Daddy appeared. We drank tea, nibbled raspberry tarts, and talked for nearly two hours...until the sun was too low for taking pictures.

"But ya'll comb back again," Mrs. M said. "Ennatime. It's fine to talk bein't it? 'N if ya comb in the spring the curtains in the bedroom will be op. We're decoratin'. 'N ya'll git a nicer picture."

Daddy took me to the backyard where Emily used to look across to Oxenhope. He pointed out the packhorse path she followed to High Sunderland Hall. He was not a fountain of Bronte lore, and I soon made my farewells. I came home by way of Luddenden Foot, stopping at the site of the railroad station where Branwell once worked. October was drawing to a close. I should be leaving Haworth soon, but one event led to the next. Nancy Fisher arrived at the Guest House. She was an American recently graduated from Radcliffe and now in England working on Charlotte Bronte's Shirley under the guiding eye of Katherine Tillotson at the University of London. On this particular (and rainy) morning I had stayed by the fire in the lounge working on accumulated notes until about 12:30 when Nancy came in from the Museum wanting to know where I was going to have lunch. I suggested Parson Lee Farm, thinking it would be a treat for her and would be an opportunity for me to pay Mrs. Wilson the shilling I still owed for the lunch she had made Pincher and me back in September.

Nancy and I drove to Wycollar and walked back the mile through the pastures to the farm. The stream was gushing from the recent rains. The rose hips and hawthorn haws were abundant along every hedge. Mrs. Wilson prepared a lunch I thought Nancy would not soon forget and again printed our check neatly on a piece of cereal box. When I presented the previous "ticket," she said, "I knew ya wooed be bok."

When I came from putting the car away that evening, George met me in the foyer. "Moor guests tonight," he said a little importantly. "Fancy ones, these. Lady Browning and her daughter will arrive before dinner."

"Lady Browning...Lady Browning," I said to myself as I climbed the stairs to my room. "That's Daphne du Maurier. Her husband, Lord Browning, is exchequer or something for the queen." Hmmm. Did I feel a tingle spiral up my spine?

I was reading in the lounge, waiting for dinner, when a woman entered and introduced herself as Oriel Vaughan. Lady Vaughan, I learned later. In the conversation that followed she admitted to being a writer. She was in Haworth to meet a friend from Cornwall.

"What have you written?" I inquired.

"Oh, nothing you would have heard of," she replied modestly. I did not pursue the subject. We talked on about writing in general until I could not resist asking, "What has your friend written?"

She looked at me a little coyly, and as much as to say "Would you believe?" replied with one word, "Rebecca?" After a brief pause, during which I could think of nothing to say beyond acknowledging I recognized the title, she added, "She's terribly shy and doesn't like to be recognized."

Lady Browning was coming to Haworth to saturate herself for a week in Bronteland, her friend told me, in preparation for writing an introduction to a new edition some publisher was bringing out of Wuthering Heights. Daphne du Maurier and I were going to share a week in the same little guesthouse? Incredible. How could I contain my excitement? But I would.

The next morning's mail brought me a letter from Sir Linton Andrews, to whom I had written when I first arrived in Haworth. As president of the Bronte Society, he was giving me permission to see any books or letters in the museum and to take "one or two pictures within the museum." In the meantime Lady Vaughan, who I concluded was companion/researcher/secretary for Lady Browning, phoned Mrs. Weir, secretary of the society, to ask permission for Lady Browning to use the material in the museum. Permission was readily granted. Then Mrs. Weir added, "There is a Miss Copeland at the guesthouse waiting to see Mr. Mitchell. I have just posted her a letter. Will you please tell her Mr. Mitchell will see you both today?" So off I trudged across the street with Daphne du Maurier, acting as though she were just another Bronte fan…like me. Once there we pursued separate interests and did not meet again until evening at dinner and then in the lounge, where the conversation swirled around the Brontes. Lady Browning declared she was "addled" by all the books folks had written about them.

"I should think," she commented, "two would do very well for Emily, Miss Ratchford's Web of Childhood and Hatfield's Complete Poems of Emily."

I noticed, though, the next evening she was reading Sparks and Stanford's The Brontes, which she later pronounced "a very balanced work…one of the best."

That weekend the guest house was full. "Unusual," George said, "for the end of October." In addition to Nancy Fisher, Lady Vaughan, Lady Browning (whom her friend called Bing), and her daughter Flavia, the guests included a German couple who had arrived on a motor bike and a photographer and his wife from Halifax, Mr. and Mrs. Waring.

Sunday morning, undaunted by the drizzle, the Warings donned their Wellingtons and macs and headed for the Waterfalls. "There's always a chance the sun will shine when we get there," Mr. Waring observed as he slung a couple of cameras over his shoulder. As for "Bing" Browning (though I would never have addressed her as such), she really wanted to go to the museum, but it didn't open until two on Sunday. "Should I ask a favor?" she pondered aloud.

"Oh, do," urged Lady Vaughan, obviously much impressed by her friend's prestige.

"We must know exactly what it is we want to ask to see. We can't waffle this." In the end, however, she decided not to ask for any favors, and the three set out for a walk on the moors.

With the approach of November, I needed to bring to a close my sojourn in Yorkshire. This rainy morning seemed a good time to plot the next steps in my literary adventure. First, I wrote the Venerable Townley, archbishop of York. He and his wife had made me promise coming over on the Queen Mary that I would spend a weekend with them when I was here. I shouldn't wait any longer. Then I wrote the Christmases, who had elicited a similar promise when I met them at a little inn in Cheshire earlier in the autumn. Another letter went to Lady Wylie, my cabin mate on the Queen Mary and widow of Lord Wylie, who had been head of the Rhodes Scholar program at Oxford. "You must come and see me when you're in Oxford," she had cajoled, and I should be in Oxford before the end of November. I would stay there until I go to Dorchester,

Dorset, for Christmas with the Hatleys. Letters to the George Eliot Society, the Folklore Society, and the English-Speaking Union needed to be written, as well, to straighten out all the higgledy-piggledy of the coming weeks.

If Daphne du Maurier wanted anonymity, she had it. One guest's activities did not infringe upon another's. That is not to say she was not friendly and outgoing. She shared opinions freely, as when she observed, "The furor over Emily has risen to such a pitch that had she been Catholic, she certainly would be canonized."

The evening I remember best we sat roasting chestnuts in the coals of the fire, my toes not six inches from Ms. du Maurier's as we reached for chestnuts cooling on the hearth. She was reading aloud from a recent issue of Transactions. Coming across a group picture of those who had attended last year's meeting of the Bronte Society, she asked, "Who in this picture would you like to spend a weekend with...and where? And why?" I could hear the wheels of a novelist whirring as she reacted one by one to our comments and encouraged all of us to react to each other. "What if...?" "What about...?" "That means you would...?" Her favorite question was "What if...?" I was listening first hand to the curiosity that must underlie the creation of a fictitious character. I would never get closer to a master spinner of plots than I was that evening sharing roasted chestnuts with Daphne du Maurier.

As the three sat at their table eating breakfast the last day of their visit, I could scarcely pretend I couldn't overhear their conversation.

"I have done everything I planned except visit High Sunderland Hall," Daphne observed. "I don't know whether that's important."

"What's there?" her daughter, Flavia, asked.

"Nothing, actually. Any more. But Emily taught school there briefly, and lived nearby at Law Hill."

"Where is it?" Lady Vaughan wanted to know.

"About ten miles from here. Not important enough to walk that far."

"What about a taxi?"

"That's a possibility. Let's finish breakfast first. Then I'll decide." As they were leaving the room a few minutes later, Ms D said to her friend, "You'd better call a taxi. If I don't go, I'll always wish I had."

At that point I butted in to say I had a car, had been to High Sunderland, had no plans for the day, and would be happy to take them to the site.

They protested. Wouldn't think of inconveniencing me. I remained noncommittal. "If you change your mind, I'll be in my room for a little while."

I had hardly finished washing out yesterday's stockings when Lady Vaughan knocked. "Bing would like to accept your offer," she said softly.

George made sandwiches and gave us a flask of coffee. Oriel added apples and chocolate. I fetched the Morris Minor, and off we chugged across the moors.

While my passengers poked around the rubble of what had once been High Sunderland Hall and thought their thoughts, I sat in the car, writing in my diary and studying the ordnance map. Finished there, Ms D did not care to get involved with Mrs. Marshall at Law Hill, and so we just skirted it and drove back onto the moors. At one point I parked the Morris and we walked down what I thought might turn into the old packhorse trail over Beacon Hill to Sunderland. But it didn't. With the picnic still intact, despite Flavia's asking, "When are we going to eat?" I drove on through Halifax to the dreary railroad station in Luddenden Foot, the latter of interest only because Branwell Bronte had worked there briefly. More accurately, he had been employed there but in truth spent more time reading and drinking beer at the Lord Nelson in Luddenden than he did working. Hence the brevity of his employment. A man at the station directed us to the Lord Nelson. The road climbed to a spectacular view. There on the top of creation, we stopped, clambered onto a "stane dyke," and enjoyed our picnic.

When the last crumbs were gone and the apple cores flung to the birds, Daphne said, "I should like to go to the Lord Nelson if we have time."

"I've plenty of time," I said casually, hoping, of course, this remarkable day would never end.

In the Lord Nelson, she found the proprietor happy to talk with us about its history. By now it was time for tea. Mr. Widdop, Ben Widdop, joined us at a table near a window overlooking the valley. He played "mother" as he launched into a bit of the history. "This was one of the first circulating libraries in Great Britain," he told us as we sipped tea. "It was started in 1781. Members of the library club paid one pound for a share in the enterprise."

"What did members get for their pound?" Lady Vaughan asked.

"Well, they used to meet once a month for two hours. I'm not privy to what they did except the records show they drew lots for turns in selecting four books to be purchased for the library each month."

"Do those records make any reference to Branwell Bronte's ever being here?" Daphne wondered.

"I don't know about the minutes of the meetings, but until four years ago the little room, which was the library, contained a chair with the label 'Branwell's Chair.'"

"Oh, that gives me goose bumps," Daphne said, shivering. "What became of it? What happened four years ago?"

"The brewery remodeled. The library nook became the gents' lav."

"And Branwell's chair?"

"Who knows?" he said, shrugging.

The conversation turned to other topics. When it came time to leave, I went with Flavia, who was picking up the tab. The other two went to spend a penny.

"Where are you from?" Mr. Widdop asked Flavia.

"We've come from Haworth today," she told him.

"I saw in the paper a famous writer's over there this week." The comment made Flavia giggle, and suddenly he realized to whom he had been talking.

She and I went on to the car without further conversation with Ben Widdop. When Daphne followed a few minutes later, she was carrying two books that had once been in the library, saying, "See what the nice man gave me." One of them she gave me as a memento of our day together. It was a three-and-a-half by-five-and-a-half leather-bound volume titled Percy Anecdotes. Inside the front cover is the library stamp and on the flyleaf in handwriting:

Luddenden Library
No. 854

Before we returned to the guesthouse, Daphne had one more request, "May we stop and walk? I haven't walked all day." So when we reached the Harbor Lodge Road leading to the peat pit, I pulled off the road and we all walked. Though I had my camera with me and would have given a good deal to have a picture of her striding through the bracken, I refrained from intruding upon her anonymity.

The sun was setting as we started back to the car. The whole horizon turned to gold. One lone mauve cloud hung over the purple moor, as we came by the tiny lake near Tom Stell's Seat.

The next morning the Keighley Professional Women were meeting their famous visitor at the railroad station when she departed to present her with a sampler of Haworth Church. I was in the lounge working on some notes when the taxi came for her and her companions.

"Thanks again," Daphne said, slipping a book under my pile of books. "If you are ever in Cornwall, come and visit." And she was gone. On the flyleaf of Rebecca she had written: "To E. Copeland with best wishes and many thanks for her company in 'Bronte' country, from Daphne du Maurier Nov. 5, 1954."

That afternoon, belatedly, Sybil and I went to the Reference Room in the Keighley Library to find out what Oriel Malet (Lady Vaughan) had written. Two of her books are Trust in the Spring Time and My Bird Sings. She was born in 1923. Her special subject is children; her interests, sailing and theater. She is the third daughter of the Earl of Lisburne, hence her title "Lady." With her departure Lady Vaughan had lost her anonymity. Sybil and I rode back to Haworth through Bolton Abbey, Burnsall, and Appletreewick. The autumn tints were lovely even in the rain.

A letter from Mrs. Townley suggested the coming weekend for a visit with her and the Venerable, but even a personal visit to York was not without its Bronte overtones. Just before Otely a sign pointed to Guiseley three-quarters of a mile to the right. I took the detour to two points of Bronte interest, the house where the Rev. Bronte first met Maria Branwell and then the parish church three miles away where they were married. By then I was lost. I stopped at a Red Lion Hotel for directions and came away with a mission.

Annie Theresa Hinchcliffe, operator, recognizing my American accent, wanted me to look up her widowed brother-in-law, valet to Baron Rothchild, on Long Island, New York, when I get home. Not sure of her intent, I didn't say "...if I don't get a better offer first."

After my visit with the Townleys (and that is a whole other story) I headed back to Haworth by way of Scarborough, admittedly out of my way by some forty miles but important for its connections with Anne Bronte. All its hotels, boarding houses, board walks, and one-way streets suggest Scarborough may be another Blackpool in summer, but that rainy November afternoon I had the beach, the castle, the streets and shops, the fog virtually to myself.

I found a bed and breakfast built on the site of where Anne once lived, two blocks from the Grand Hotel. After registering (for ten and sixpence a night), I made my pilgrimage to Anne's grave. It was completely covered with pansies, one little purple blossom bobbing in the rain. Obviously someone, probably from the Bronte Society, provides tender, loving care for the site. Not far away Castle Hill Road leads to the castle on a high cliff, extending far out into the North Sea. I stood and watched the beach far, far below on either side. It had a Bronte mood. Magnificent and drear. I bought a picnic basket at Boots the Chemist, my going away gift for the Shuttleworths, and returned to my B & B.

The next morning I walked along Anne's beach. The day was beautiful after yesterday's rain. I bought a yellow rose at a corner florist shop, took it to Anne's grave, and placed it among the pansies.

My meandering route back to Haworth started with Rivaulx Abbey, beautiful ruins, a photographer's delight on such a gorgeous day. Fortunately I had a good supply of film. After a day of ruins and churches—Bylan Abbey, Coxwald Church with a flag flying atop its octagonal tower, and Shandy Hill just beyond—I reached Jervaulx Abbey about sunset. My guidebook described Jervaulx as "a bit pathetic" in comparison with Rivaulx, but arriving at my favorite time of day, I found Jervaulz an enchanted spot. The sun was setting as a full moon rose, rabbits scampered over centuries-old gravestones, a pheasant whirred through the cloisters. Tiny purple flowers blossomed on a vine covering the abbey walls. Autumn tints were rusty in the fading light, and a hawthorn bush silhouetted against white wispy clouds created artistic designs. An old monk stirred in his grave. Then all was quiet except for the chomp, chomp of cows nibbling in the pasture. As I left the grounds, a pink sunset flooded the sky with two deep splashes off to the north. A Scottish gamekeeper tramped across his Yorkshire property.

Earlier in the day I had reserved a room at the Old Deanery Hotel opposite the Minster in Ripon, planning to visit Fountains Abbey the next morning. A smiling waiter served a chicken dinner in a spic-and-span, flower-filled dining room. It wasn't crowded and he was feeling sociable. He had been born in Halifax, Nova Scotia, he told me, where he lived until he was eight. Had spent his life working, first on ships and then railroads, retiring at sixty-five to Ripon. Now in retirement he was waiting on tables in Ripon, the town where the watchman blows his horn in the market place each night at nine. But at nine I was snug by the lounge fire listening to the Minster bells. Soon after, I went to bed between clove-scented sheets.

Fountains Abbey was to have completed my abbey splurge, but the rain was torrential when I reached the West Gate. Ward Lock says, "Fountains is the most noble of the lot..." and extensive. This was not the day, though, for me to visit. I drove on to Pately Bridge, where I stopped for elevenses of coffee and crumpet.

With my departure from Haworth finally set for three days hence, I decided to accept the Standishes' offer for a full-day tour of places within a radius of some thirty miles, all towns and hamlets I had not yet visited but which were some way related to the Brontes. We would make it a farewell party day and celebrate Sybil's birthday at the same time. In Gomersall we visited Red House, a lovely brick home, supposedly the model Charlotte chose for the home of the Yorkes in Shirley. On we drove through Birstall, Spenborough, to Harthead where Rev. Bronte lived when he was curate there. George knew the area well, though he had not been in some of these villages in thirty years. Rydings, Liveridge, Murfield—he knew the history of them all. Somewhere on a narrow, unfenced road between Hubberholme and Hawes we stopped beside the road for Sybil's birthday picnic of sausage pie, polony, gooseberry tarts, and dry fly. The sunny day gave way to a bucketsful rain before we reached home, even snow swirled around us as we crossed the moortops.

When I read the Daily Telegraph the next morning I expected any moment to hear Macduff burst into the room shouting, "Confusion now hath made his masterpiece! Most sacrilegious murder hath broke ope the Lord's anointed temple..." for according to the morning paper the night had been "unruly." The headlines read, "Floods and Gales Damage Homes: Traffic Delayed," "Chimney Stack Kills Widow," "Worst Roads in Thirty Years at Hull." One man lost his life when his coattail caught in the works of a clock. Winds at Clyde reached 100 miles an hour. A mother and two children escaped injury when a chimney stack crashed through their roof. A car was caught and overturned by a flash flood and all three occupants drowned...telephones out of order...water as high as letter boxes...a fourteen-ton tree blocked a main road for hours. The Britannic was delayed from docking for five hours. Yet the British tell me they are glad they do not live in New England where we have hurricanes.

The weather cleared by afternoon, though the wind was still strong, but oh, so soft. Pincher bounced in anticipation when I took his leash from the hook, and we started off. For my last stroll on the moors until I didn't know when, I set out for Penistone Crag and its Fairy Cave, by way of Ponden Hall. The wind subsided and I grew warmer as I climbed the lane to the path along Ponden Clough. The crag itself, an outcropping from the moor, stood about thirty feet tall at the end of the clough. From its base a steep path climbs up and along the edge to the moors themselves. About a third of the way up is the Fairy Cave, a

Penistone Crag

and its Fairy Cave

ledge within the crag. It stretches about twelve feet from end to end, varies in width from two to three feet, and…aye, here's the rub, is not more than two feet from ledge to overhanging rock. Being open at both ends, it is more of an open-sided tunnel than a cave. This, according to local lore, is where "they marry the odd 'uns." That is, an unmarried woman who manages to wiggle through the space and back again should marry within the year. However, my accomplishing the feat has disproved the maxim. This is where Catherine and Heathcliffe often came to play as children in Wuthering Heights.

I stood a long time beside the Fairy Cave, looking back along the bracken path below me, across the reservoir to Thrushcross Grange and beyond to Stanbury in the distance. To my left a boy and his dog were gamboling on the moor. Heathcliffe, perhaps, reincarnated? But where was Catherine? Turning then, I headed up and across the pathless moor, knowing I would emerge at the top to look down upon Upper Withins. I didn't miss my mark by much. There slightly to my left was the tumbled down farm and lone tree, the object of my first walk on the moors back in September. The purple heather-bell was now gone, but Emily's line came to me: "such wild notes wake these passes lone." I followed the well-worn path down from the Heights, stopping at the Silent Inn in Stanbury for a sandwich and strawberry mineral before returning to the guest house.

After tea I strolled up the lane to the Shuttleworth's, arriving in time to hear "The Northcountryman" on the wireless. A man talked about the dialect, the inconsistency of broad and short a's, sometimes even within one sentence. And he told a story of a Yorkshire man and his wife who went to a country fair to celebrate their twenty-fifth wedding anniversary. Someone at the fair offered five pounds to anyone who would walk the tight rope. The wife volunteered, walked it, and collected. The husband said, "Aye, luv, 'n tha niver told me tha could walk a tight rope." "Nae, luv," she replied. "Tha niver asked."

I had met Mrs. Shuttleworth the first day I arrived in Haworth. She was returning from the bakery with oatcakes for their tea. I was interested because Emily Bronte describes oatcakes hanging on a rack in Thrushcross Grange. I was as puzzled as my students as to why they were hanging on a rack. And what exactly were oatcakes anyway? And what kind of rack? During my visit in Haworth, Mrs. Shuttleworth had let me take pictures of oatcakes hanging on her kitchen rack, the wooden arms of which are raised and lowered by a pulley. It was the sort of rack I can remember from my childhood my mother had in the kitchen to air clothes on after she had ironed them. Mr. Feather, owner of the Bronte Bakery, hearing of my interest in oatcakes, invited me to visit the bakery someday when he was making oatcakes.

On my last full day in Haworth, I took Mr. Feather up on his invitation. I set out early (8:30 is early in Britain). The day was crisp and frosty, alive with people walking to the factories at the bottom of the hill. Green hills and

Looking back to the path below

Oatcakes on a Rack

gray stone walls poked through the valley mist. Everyone had a "gone mornen" or "cauld day" for me. Folks seemed to be speaking more clearly than when I first arrived. I recalled overhearing someone ask in a shop early in my visit, "Dewsiligs?" Yes, they sold eggs. The school bell rang in the hollow and children, many in clogs, rushed along the lane through the park.

Mr. Feather said if I could stay a bit he'd let me throw the last oatcakes. But mind, I should watch him carefully as he progressed to the bottom of the "two stone" bowl. He mixes the batter using Dunfermlaine flour the night before, gets up at five o'clock the next morning, heats his two coal grills to five hundred degrees, and starts baking nineteen dozen oatcakes. Mrs. Feather came in with a cup of tea for me in time to enjoy the joke when I "threw" the next-to-the-last oatcake quite unsuccessfully. It had looked so simple when Mr. Feather did it. He put a daub of batter on the grill and then pulled a handle, which propelled a roller across the batter leaving what greatly resembled a large, thin pizza crust. Mine was still just a lump of batter. Putting more strength behind the next throw, I had a little more success. The oatcake at that stage is limp like a raw pizza crust, hence the need to hang it to dry before tea time when it is broken into pieces and served crisp with farmers' cream and jam. I certainly left the bakery with considerable respect for the muscle that produces nineteen dozen oatcakes in one morning.

By the time I had climbed back up the hill, said goodbye to the Shuttleworths and given them the picnic basket I had bought for them in Scarborough, and won the bet with George that I could get everything (well, almost everything) into my footlocker and suitcase, it was time to say goodbye. Sybil insisted upon an early farewell tea of toasted pikelets (Yorkshire crumpets) before the lounge fire. Pincher's suspicions were confirmed when he saw the trunk come sliding down the red and blue carpeted stairs. With promises to come back in the spring, I was on my way to Cheadle Hulme seven miles south of Manchester to spend a few days with Mary and Edgar Christmas on my way to Oxford.

The Merry Christmases

(diary excerpt)
Cheadle Hulme, Cheshire
November 16, 1954

There was something very cordial about Mrs. Christmas's open arms and the way she said, "Oh, good! You've come in time to chat before John comes home. Chris is waiting for you by the fire." Chris, Mr. Christopher, had all his stomach muscles torn out in a World War I injury, the only man, his wife told me, to survive such damage. Five times since then he has been carried off to a hospital "for the last time," suffering from strangulation, but each time he has come back. He was having a bad day today; he had ridden too far into the Peaks with son John on Sunday. But difficult breathing didn't keep him from telling me long stories this evening about Yorkshire frankness, friendship and individuality.

John works in the personnel department of a Manchester factory and his brother Jimmy, at Thomas Cooke & Sons. As soon as they made their boisterous and quiet, respectively, entrances, we sat down to a chutney pie supper, which turned out to be an inquisition concerning life in America, carried on mostly by John.

Mum and Dad told the boys, though I am sure they had heard the story before, how we met in a quiet little lounge a couple of months before. If I hadn't finally asked a question, we probably would have sat there the rest of the evening in silence, but once the silence was broken nothing could shut us off until an hour or so later, when I decided to retire. And we laughed, recalling the elderly woman (not privy to our party), who was there with her son and daughter-in-law, and who broke the silence of the entire lounge when I stood to leave. In the audible stage whisper of the hard of hearing, she said to her son, "She looks a lot bigger standing up."

I knew John was bursting to drive my Morris Minor, and so after supper I offered him the keys and said, "Go to it!" He soon returned, pronouncing,

"It corners well." Then he and Jimmy played Gilbert and Sullivan for me on the gramophone. Mr. Christmas lent me A Sea of Silence for my bedtime reading.

Cheadle Hulme
November 17, 1954

"This bright and sunny spot belongs to me," I hummed to myself as I parked the car on a grassy plot a mile from Pott Shrigly in one direction and a mile from Adlington Hall in the other. I wanted to visit Adlington Hall where Handel had once lived, but a sign on the door read, "Closed until Good Friday, 1955." The estate office nearby unyieldingly verified the statement. Now in this sunny spot I am writing up my diary for the past two days, looking over the map in anticipation of my next move and nibbling digestive biscuits with Stilton cheese.

At 9:30 this morning Mrs. Christmas brought a tray of tea and thin-sliced bread and butter. "Snooze another hour or so," she said, "while I get Chris fixed up. He's staying in bed today." It was easy to snooze and browse in A Sea of Silence. How will I ever adjust to going to work again next September! At the ten o'clock bacon-and-egg breakfast, Mrs. Christmas and I chatted. In explaining why she would have to be out this evening—"John is thrilled to have you to himself"—she went into a rather detailed and very interesting account of how she and Chris had become Christian Scientists. She feels sure their faith has brought Chris home five times from strangulations doctors decreed fatal. The boys have been brought up on Christian Science and Mrs. C thinks their religion accounts for the sons' cheerful, wholesome outlook on life. Mrs. C is a reader for her group every Wednesday and Sunday.

"Do get back for a nice tea before John comes home," Mrs. C had said as I started out on this day of hunting for Halls. After a sunny interval at the cross roads, I drove on, with some confusion of roads, to Lyme Hall, for six hundred years the home of the Leighs until in 1946 Sir Newton Leigh gave the 1,340-acre estate to the National Trust. The park was full of sheep and deer this afternoon. I was the only visitor in the guided tour of Grinling Gibbons's carvings and James II's apartment of the original blue and maroon embossed wallpaper and fascinating furnishings.

In the evening John took me to see Three Coins in the Fountain.

Cheadle Hulme
November 18, 1954

This epicurean life will never do. Mrs. Christmas brought my tea at 9:15, said it was a messy day outside and that I should stay in bed at least another hour, and then have a leisurely bath and brunch. Who am I to defy my hostess? After breakfast I went upstairs to chat with Mr. Christmas, who is staying in bed until his breathing gets back to normal. He said I neglected him yesterday, but I teased him about Diana, a neighbor who spent the evening with him. She is a close friend of the family, and John is godfather to her seven-month-old daughter, Nichola. John made coffee and Welsh rarebit for us all after we came from the cinema last evening.

Diana became so interested in my literary travels she invited me to see her books today. "But you should see the children also," Mrs. C said.

"Not both at once, though," Diana said defensively. Consequently, I made two visits to Diana today—one for nursery tea with Mrs. C, Diana, Nicky, and three-year-old Michael, returning to the Christmases for steak and liver and onions, baked apples 'n things and then back to Diana's with Johnny and Jim MacPhearson—Glasgow to the bone—for books, sausage rolls, Ovaltine, and roasted chestnuts. Diana's husband Peter is in a business that requires long trips on the continent, buying waste cotton. He is in Germany right now.

But back to my visit with Mr. Christmas this morning. We ran the gamut of subjects from his Yorkshire unit in the 14-18 War that wouldn't fight until it was issued clogs, the movie John and I saw last night, travel in Italy and Mrs. C's sister who nursed King Farouk when he was a baby. She has often wondered whether she did right to let him live. We talked also of the Stanley Expedition of which Mr. Christopher's father was a member.

But this holiday from holidays cannot last. I will force myself to say goodbye to my hospitable new friends, the Christmases.

George Eliot

(diary excerpt)
Nuneaton, Warwickshire
November 19, 1954

This afternoon I crossed the Peaks from Macclesfield to Buxton into Lichfield, where Samuel Johnson's name came first to mind. The Peaks must be beautiful, I judged, from lack of distracting civilization and the occasional lay-bys, but as I climbed, the fog settled in, limiting visibility to about fifty feet. Therefore, I cannot vouch for anything except the helpful white dashes in the middle of the road.

Johnson's Lichfield was also enshrouded in fog, making the cathedral spire look ethereal. And graceful, after so many northern towers I had seen. Northamptonshire is known as "the shire of spires and squires." Other northern churches almost invariably have towers instead of spires. The crumbling stone of the north does not lend itself to pointed spires.

In Nuneaton I found the Newdegate Arms Hotel where Mr. Twigger, Hon. Secretary of the George Eliot Fellowship, had made a reservation for me. A letter from Mr. Twigger had announced he would call at seven to welcome me. From recent correspondence I had expected a rather seasoned and mustached gentleman of the old school. His extreme youth gave me a bit of a startle. We chatted in the lounge for an hour, during which time I learned he is the youngest secretary of the Eliot Fellowship on record and is also secretary of the local Literary and Debating Society. By virtue of this tie he succeeded in bringing the two groups together last Monday, a major achievement, as the Fellowship feels the Society does not pay enough attention to Eliot, and the Society feels that Burton's Anatomy of Melancholy and Drayton and countless other local writers deserve as much attention as does George Eliot.

Before we parted for the evening, Mr. Twigger telephoned the Hon. L.C.S. Fitzroy Newdegate to see whether we could visit Arbury Hall tomorrow. Permission granted.

Nuneaton, Warwickshire
November 20, 1954

Mary Ann Evans, who later took the pen name George Eliot, was born on the Aubury Estate, where her father was estate agent. It has been the home of the Newdegates since the sixteenth century. Two years ago (1952) it was turned over to the National Trust; however, the family still lives there. The Hall and gardens are open to the public in the summer, but not in November. Mr. Twigger, with his exuberance, pointed out that I had come from the Brontes and was on my way to Thomas Hardy, and pleaded, "Let's give George Eliot an American break." The result, we would be received at 2:30 P.M. this afternoon.

The George Eliot Fellowship is young and struggling. I gathered it does not have much clout with the town fathers. Started in 1930, it was barely breathing when World War II disrupted activities, but it resolved never to rest until a suitable memorial was erected to George Eliot. And the first act of the postwar Town Council Planning Committee was to approve the George Eliot Memorial and Gardens on a bombed-out site on Church Street. The gardens were opened two years ago.

The Fellowship planned recently to mount a George Eliot exhibit at the Bedworth Methodist Bazaar. Only after publicity went out did they find they could not get enough together for the exhibit. Coventry would not lend things for a church hall, nor would the local library. Mr. Twigger has a flannel he believes was used for cleaning silver, "but that is hardly an exhibit," he said, sighing.

Mr. Twigger went with me for our 2:30 appointment with Mrs. Newdegate at the Aubury Estate where she showed me the gallery and the chapel with the carving of Grinling Gibbons, though there is some doubt as to its authenticity. The work is inferior and lacks the open peapod, his trademark. The fan-vaulted ceilings are impressive, though Mr. Twigger says they give him architectural indigestion. We were brought abruptly to the present when we moved to the drawing room and dining room where today's grouse hunters were gathering for lunch.

Nuneaton, Warwickshire
November 21, 1954

The remembrance weekend for George Eliot, which had brought me to Nuneaton at this time, began with our being led to the obelisk in the George Eliot Gardens by the mayor of Nuneaton, Councillor Mrs. L. Whetstone. The mayor placed a wreath on the memorial, someone read brief passages from several of Eliot's books and Canon Herbert said a prayer. Then a coach took us to St. Paul's Church in Stockingford for a church service. The Rev.

Taylor's text was "Gather up the fragments that remain that nothing may be lost" (John 6:12). He spoke first of the hundred-year-old custom of harvest festivals and commented that he had never seen the harvest of the mind represented at these festivals. That observation led him to his tribute to George Eliot with special allusions to her use of this church in her works.

I learned later at tea that Mr. Twigger had asked a Mrs. Dodds to be nice to me. Mrs. Dodds, "friend and collaborator" of Professor Gordon S. Haight and the best local authority of George Eliot, sat with me in church near the memorial tablet to Rev. J.E. Jones (Rev. Edgar Tryan in Janet's Repentance) and asked me home to tea along with Miss Lyons of the Coventry Library. Mr. Dodds is son of Matthew Arnold Dodds, canon of Coventry and vicar of Chilvers Coton Church from 1914 until his death in 1928. The old vicarage (Scenes of Clerical Life) has been torn down but the present Mr. Dodds lived in it as a boy. Mrs. Dodds spent the evening showing me clippings, books and relics of George Eliot. She has a piece of blotting paper from G.E.'s desk with G.E.'s neat purple signature and the baby bonnet of Rev. B.G. Ebdell (Mr. Gilful) and his clerical bands.

Nuneaton, Warwickshire
November 22, 1954

The day started with Mrs. Dodds's personally conducted tour of Chilvers Coton (Shepperton) Church. Around Nuneaton things and people are as likely to be called by their name in Eliot's fiction as by their real name. The Chilvers Coton Church, aside from its own history, has an intriguing story of its recent (1947) reconstruction by sixteen talented German prisoners of war in seventeen months. Working with the crudest implements they salvaged a remarkable amount of the church that had been destroyed by bombs in 1941. Most of the wood was burned, but they dressed down enough of what was left to panel the altar end of the church. The altar itself is made of pieces from the original. Around the pulpit and font are lovely carvings that some of the prisoners did. The wooden, carved plaques of religious scenes look more German than British, but very right for the little church.

Mrs. Newdegate is lay rector of the parish. The Newdegates have been lay rectors ever since Aubry Hall was a priory. They personally select the vicar of the parish. Until this reconstruction the Newdegates have owned the chancel of the church, but now Mrs. Newdegate has given it to be used by the choir, keeping only one small space, with the Newdegate lion's foot (called leopard by G. E.) with the coat of arms, where she sits on special occasions. Interesting to me, since I had met him, Mr. Dodds has been organist here since he was able to reach the pedals of the organ. A real organ has just been given and dedicated.

This is the first time I have had the American flag raised in my honor. But at the George Eliot banquet tonight, the Eliot portrait was draped on one side by the British flag and the other by the American flag. The chairman told me afterward that this is the second time they have used the flag at an Eliot dinner. Last year Dr. Haight of Yale was here working on the letters. The Letters, the first three volumes of a proposed six, have just been published. Mrs. Dodds has a complimentary set inscribed "to Dorothy Dodds, friend and collaborator."

After the Cheltenham literature dinner, I knew what to expect this evening, and though dressier, this one was less formal and more relaxed. Miss Lyons, whom I had met at Mrs. Dodds's tea yesterday, was waiting for me in the cloak room, and I did know Mrs. Fitzroy Newdegate in the receiving line.

Remembering all the toasts we had "prayed silence" for at the Cheltenham Literary Festival and now the ones at the George Eliot banquet, I commented to Alice Lyons on the popularity of toasting in Britain.

"That reminds me," she said. "Would you be willing to give the toast in response to the toast to guests at our annual Soroptomists meeting in Coventry next spring?"

"Tell me first, what is a soroptomist?"

"It is an international organization. You must have chapters in America. We are a do-good sort of folk."

"Let me think about it," I said. "I'll let you know within a few weeks when I see how my travels are going to shape up for spring." And we left it at that.

Miss Powell

MIDWAY THROUGH MY Atlantic crossing on HMS Queen Mary a flighty little lady interrupted my letter writing in the tourist lounge, asking tentatively, "Can you count?" Wondering whether the question was more complicated than it sounded, I hesitated. Before I could reply, she added, "Can you count, umm, canasta?" When I admitted I could, she added, "Will you play with us? Canasta?" That is how I came to meet Miss Powell of Surrey, Mrs. Harper of Dallas, and Miss Spittal (accent on second syllable, please) of Glasgow. We played canasta in a congenial, shipmately way until Miss Powell declared it was four o'clock and time for tea. She and Miss Spittal went off to find a place for four.

Miss Spittal returned first, announcing, "There is only one chair."

"But there is room for four," Miss Powell added as she approached with a kind of anything-is-possible air.

"But it won't do," insisted Miss Spittal, the Scot.

"There is a pregnant woman with a little girl saving the place for us." This from Miss Powell.

"It's no use. There isn't room."

So the Brit and the Scot tossed it back and forth until the wraithlike Miss Powell said in a soft voice, "Follow me," with such conviction we all followed unquestioningly. And we all had tea.

I did not see Miss Powell again until after we left Cherbourg two days later. All luggage and cars destined for France had been hoisted ashore, and passengers for that port had departed. Southampton would be next. All that was left to do was exchange addresses with the friends we had made so quickly and eternally during the five days at sea. I was scanning the channel for the first glimpse of Southampton when Miss Powell found me again. She said, "I want you to have my address. Call me when you come to London. Perhaps I can do something for you." Glancing at the address, I saw it was simply Hampton Court, East Molesey, Surrey.

I took the boat train to London and that evening caught the Flying Scotsman for Edinburgh. For the next four months my literary peregrinations in pursuit of Bobby Burns, Macbeth, the Bronte sisters, and the Lake poets kept me in the North and so filled my days that I did not return to London until after Christmas. Although the Hatleys, with whom I spent Christmas in Dorchester, insisted I should stay for Twelfth Night festivities, I felt London at last was calling. They had spoiled me too much already.

In London I took a room in a bed and breakfast inn on Grenville Place off Cromwell Road for five pounds a week. The first task was to register my Morris Minor with the London City Council at the south end of Westminster Bridge. I did not plan to drive for a couple of months, but I wanted all forms in order should a contingency arise. So across Westminster Bridge I walked to the Council offices. I was first sent upstairs for the special application needed by all license markers ending in D. Until then I did not know I was coded. Back downstairs I queued for the cashier before I could queue for my license. Welcome to the London Queue.

The Thames was ghostly quiet when I emerged onto the Embankment. The lights of Whitehall blurred through the fog. Back across Westminster Bridge, I set out to get some city streets straight in my mental compass. With Big Ben and Parliament buildings on my left, I turned right and walked along Whitehall between the Horse Guards and Scotland Yard to Trafalgar Square. At Haymarket I stopped at American Express to pick up mail.

Light fades early in a London winter. The sun sets at four o'clock. Though it was only four-thirty, it was nearly dark when I came upon the Diaghilev Exhibition at Forbes House near Hyde Park Corner. There was plenty of time to tarry before the theater that evening. Inside were fourteen galleries of ballet paintings in tribute to Diaghilev. Music commissioned or used by him was being broadcast throughout the exhibit. One especially magnificent room, devoted entirely to portraits, sparkled with crystal chandeliers reflected in floor-to-ceiling mirrors at each end of the hall. The last room was a dimly lit hall where one could sit and listen to music. A fire sparked and leaped in an ornate fireplace. I sat, contemplating the fate that had brought me to this place at this time. It was New Year's Eve, and I felt like Alice in Wonderland.

Theater is for children at Christmastime in Great Britain. Toad of Toad Hollow, Mother Goose, The Nutcracker Suite—all are perennials. Toad was playing at Prince's Theatre in High Holborn, just the right chaser for Diaghilev. Pure charm and fantasy. For a moment I wondered whether I needed a child to gain admission. Much of my enjoyment that evening was watching children's amazed absorption in Toad's antics.

I had intended to welcome in the new year with a service at St. Paul's Cathedral, but emerging from the theater at ten o'clock to find crowds gathering in Piccadilly Circus, I opted for the outdoor activities. I walked on to

Trafalgar Square where, I once heard, revelers at the stroke of twelve leap into the Trafalgar pool. And, sure enough, as the first stroke of Big Ben boomed, several fully clothed youths jumped into the water, pulling their reluctant girlfriends with them. They romped in the fountains' spray, the girls squealing and shrieking.

A letter from home earlier in the day said that Dad and Mom would be thinking of me when Big Ben rang out the old and in the new. It was comforting to know I was in touch (or at least in sound) with my family across the ocean when 1955 dawned, though I was sound asleep at Dawson's Private Hotel on Grenville Place by the time the New Year reached Connecticut.

New Year's Day I walked and walked, continuing to put the London jigsaw together: up Regent past Weatherall's, Jaeger's, Liberty's, and Dickens and Jones. Regent Street was bustling with holidayers. Most stores were closed. I turned left into Conduit Street and found my way crosslots to Park Lane. I walked the length of Park Lane to a Charles Dickens exhibit in the House of Bawley at Number 135, complete with Dickens himself in wax, sitting at his desk. Leaving Number 135, I turned right onto Oxford and continued to Holborn.

On Dean Street in Soho the Tyrol Restaurant tempted me to a holiday lunch. Great, carved Austrian figures decorated the walls of the dining room. The waiters, similarly attired, bobbed and served as smoothly as they might schuss a Tyrolian slope. Tasty potted shrimp preceded steak, spinach, and too many potato chips, which at home would have been called French fries. The basket of fresh, warm Austrian brown bread left little room for dessert, which was Pear Helene—a scoop of vanilla ice cream, capped with a pear half, covered with chocolate sauce, and surrounded with whipped cream rosettes. Very pretty. A walk down Old Compton to Piccadilly worked off some of the calories.

At Oxford Circle I took the tube to St. Paul's Cathedral for the four o'clock service. The point of the sermon was that Christmas does not begin in October, as shopkeepers seem to think, but rather on Christmas Eve. The proper time to celebrate is after the baby is born. A choral program followed the sermon, mostly sung by the St. Paul's Boys' Choir with the congregation joining in on "The First Noel" and "Oh, Come, All Ye Faithful." Sitting directly under the massive dome and not far from the choir, I found my mind frequently wandering from the service to my surroundings.

• • •

When the cold comes, "What will poor robin do then, poor thing?" Why, put another shilling in the gas fireplace, of course, wrap up in a Macbeth tartan, and settle down with a good book. Major Stevens pointed out when I rented the room that the quiet of looking out on the garden would be well worth the extra ten shillings a week over the ground floor on the front. He left the choice, however, between a large or small room—both with garden views—up to me. Without a moment's hesitation I chose the larger one. I like space. Having never experienced gas fireplaces, I had no way of knowing how many shillings a large room could eat on a cold day.

The weather forecast for January 4 was "Cold west winds in most areas. Showers in the North. Snow and sleet in the South. Sunrise, 8:05 A.M. Sunset, 4:05 P.M." Soon I learned what the Hatleys meant when they said the east wind is deadly. The east wind kills the gardens, turns the Brussel sprouts black, and blows the Hatleys' living room rug up and down as they sit by the fire. I was reminded of arguments between Glasgow and Edinburgh residents last September as to whether the wind is kindlier in one city than the other. The consensus was it is kindlier in the city you are not in. Well, at least my rug did not flutter as I read by the fire.

I smelled the snow before I stuck my nose out of my sleeping bag. The garden below lay covered in white. Flakes were still falling. A few hardy Brits, scarves flying, heads bent against the wind, strode past frosted flowerbeds. A squirrel made scrimshaw tracks from park bench to park bench. Tree branches, outlined in sticky snow, were beginning to loop. By the time Bridget brought my eggs and bacon, fried bread, toast, and marmalade, I had stoked the fire with shillings and declared a storm holiday to work on a manuscript to accompany the pictures I took in Scotland for an article on Bobby Burns.

Midafternoon, though, found me frequently peering over my glasses into the garden, mentally measuring the depth of the snow and wondering whether I should go to Erna Low's Travel Agency to book for winter sports on the Continent. By four o'clock I could resist the snow no longer. It was nearly dark, I needed to stretch, and my fire might run out of shillings before bedtime.

At the Lyons bakery on the corner, I bought two rolls and asked for shillings in change, but the bakery had no shillings. At a second bakery I bought two scones, again asking for shillings with the same result. I next went to the post office and forthrightly asked for a pound's worth of shillings. "We've had a dreadful run on shillings all day," the postman explained apologetically, handing me the last one in his till. The clerk at the next window had one to match that one. And so I arrived back at my room with two rolls, two scones, two shillings, and two red cheeks, invigorated by my tramp in the snow.

The evening paper told about blizzards and twelve-foot drifts in southern England, but the four or six inches of snow in my garden was too wet to drift. The paper also ran a short blurb about the shilling shortage in this crisis. One bank was limiting its customers to five shillings per person. My solution was to find somewhere else to do my reading on a stormy day.

To that end the next day I went to the London Library to inquire about reading privileges and learned it costs ten guineas a year for a proper membership, which would allow me to take out up to fifteen books at a time for one or two months. However! For ten-shillings-six a month I could have a temporary membership, which would give me the run of the library—stacks and all—with reading to be done in a cozy reading room with comfortable chairs by a roaring fire. That, I decided, would suit me just fine.

I spent the rest of the afternoon browsing in the biography stacks, finding plenty of Wordsworth and Jane Austin to keep me busy for a long time, but I am going to start with Charles Dickens. A Week's Ramble in Dickens Land, though published in 1891, will give me a lead on where to go for pictures when spring comes.

Major Stevens, my landlord, stopped me one morning as I was headed for the library. He asked whether I had met his wife. I had. "She's getting the daughter ready to return to school," he informed me. "You know about the British system of education? We bear children and send them off to school so we see them only six weeks out of fifty-two until they grow up and leave home anyway."

"But they do get educated," I said consolingly.

"I wonder! My daughter told me the other day she doesn't know what a split infinitive is." Umm! I didn't ask whether he told her.

A few minutes later in the Gloucester tube station, a man gripped my elbow. Turning to see whether someone was being fresh, I gazed into those brown Yorkshire eyes of George Standish, proprietor of the Bronte Guest House. "George!" I exclaimed. "How great to see you. Where have you come from? And where are you going?"

"The Mrs.," he explained, "is phoning her sister Ivy. We arrived in London just yesterday from a month in Spain. Had a wonderful time, of course. One does, doesn't one?"

"We did it all in coaches," Sybil said when she joined us. "Wish we'd had your car." Nothing would do but to find somewhere to have a spot of tea and a good old chinwag. Their daughter Kathleen was in London, taking a nursing course out near Paddington.

"You must call her. Give 'er the number, Syb," George said. With tea finished we had to part, they to visit sister Ivy and I to keep my rendezvous with Dickens.

Is it the schoolteacher in me that makes me love libraries? I inhale deeply, nurturing my soul. From the stacks I moved to the reading room. I have never been in a genuine, honest-to-goodness London Club, but I wonder whether the London Library is not one, of sorts. Except that "silence is requested" in the Reading Room. On one side of me this morning in one of the big leather chairs that encircle the roaring fire sat an elegantly dressed, deaf-aided gentleman who looked as though he might live in one of the stately homes of England. He was reading Punch and ur-umphing rather frequently—and audibly. I wondered whether the man sitting on the other side of me in a morning suit was a bridegroom waiting for a wedding or a waiter from a Lyons Corner House until he dropped his paper and started snoring. I decided against bridegroom.

In Dorchester over Christmas, allusions to so much as heavy, relaxed breathing in the presence of one's own family in the living room of one's own home led me to believe the lapse most rude and unforgivable. Not so in the London Library, where no stigma seems attached to unrestrained snoring on a wintry afternoon.

I had been in London over two weeks. I had seen Lilli Palmer and Rex Harrison in Bell, Book and Candle, Peggy Ashcroft in Heda Gabler, Eli Wallach in Tea House of the August Moon, Ruth Gordon in The Matchmaker, John Neville in Richard II, and a few other plays. I had attained a student's pass to the Reading Room of the British Museum. I had seen The Marriage of Figaro at the Covent Garden Opera, attended concerts at Sadler's Wells, Albert Hall, and the royal Festival Hall, and sampled enough restaurants to know the difference between a Teddy Bear Picnic and a Knickerbocker Glory. Then as I was eating breakfast in front of my gas fire one morning, I asked, "What's missing? Except, of course, my family and friends back home?" For four months before coming to London, I had lived in homes. I boarded with Miss Kenneth in Edinburgh. The Bronte Guest House usually had two or three other guests with whom I chatted over café au lait in the evening. And the Standishes themselves treated me like family. Helen Layton adopted me in Oxford, where I shared her home, as did the Hatleys in Dorchester. What was missing was the opportunity for some good conversation, someone to exchange ideas with about the plays I had seen, the concerts I had attended. I had been so caught up in exploring London I had made no effort to make friends.

Ken Phelps, the maverick Bronte addict, who said in October he would meet me on the eighteenth step of the British Museum on the eighteenth of January, was true to his word. There (in the museum, not on the eighteenth step) we browsed over the miniature books the Bronte children wrote when they were little and some of Emily's poetry. Ken was as enthusiastic and informative about the Brontes as he had been in Haworth. When he asked how I happened to pick the eighteenth out of the blue to meet him at the museum three months before I came to London, I confessed it was my birthday. He accused me of being a scheming rogue but took me out to dinner anyway.

Helen Layton had come up once from Oxford for lunch and a visit to an art exhibit in the Burlington Arcade. So I was not exactly friendless, but the time had come to expand my circle of acquaintances. Otherwise, I might spend the next two months talking mostly with elevator operators, theater ushers, and the maid who brought breakfast to my room each morning. A letter from Mr. Carpenter, whose name I had been given at the English-Speaking Union, had just come in the morning's mail, saying he goes to the Jane Austen House in Chawton every Thursday, weather permitting. He added he is seventy-four and that an east wind will sometimes keep him indoors. He invited me to join him whenever I like. I will surely accept his offer.

Then I remembered Miss Powell and her, saying, "I may be able to do something for you." I wondered what. I promptly posted a note saying I was at last in London. Could we meet for tea? Three days later came her reply, "Call and set a time and place for lunch on Thursday next." I phoned that evening, and we agreed to meet at Lyons Salad Bowl. The next morning she rang up, saying, "We may not recognize each other. I shall wear a black coat. And shall I add a red or white flower?" She would wear a white flower.

I was early, but Miss Mary Lynette Powell was waiting when I arrived. On the lapel of her black coat was pinned a paper camellia from her New York visit. But I would have recognized her anyway.

"Let us ask for a quiet table where we can dine in leisure," she said, as we entered the restaurant. When she slipped off her coat, with its white camellia, her slim, five-foot-one body (maybe five-foot) was dwarfed in a long gray cardigan. Her salt-and-pepper perm, defying both bobby pins and pill-box hat, gave the appearance of being perpetually wind blown. Her soft gray eyes met my gaze warmly, belying an outward reserve. I have called her flighty. On the Queen Mary I thought her scattered-brained, but really she is neither. Jumpy, maybe, but jumpy like a hummingbird. She hovers, surveying, wings moving so fast she appears to be motionless. Then she darts, straight to the situation at hand. She's a mover. Not a king maker, but a mover. Need a fourth for canasta? She will find one. Want a nice place for tea? She will find one. Need a friend? She will find one.

"What have you been doing since we parted in August?" she asked after we had studied the menu and the waitress had taken our orders.

"I've followed the story of Macbeth from Cawdor Castle to Dunsinane and pursued Emily Bronte from birthplace to graveyard. What about you?"

"Dunsinane," she pondered. "Do you think Shakespeare himself ever went to Dunsinane?"

"Probably not. He needed only to know a place existed to use it in a play. But a picture of that great crag in the Sidlaws, which Scots call King's Seat and Shakespeare called Dunsinane, may illustrate to students back in the States how a dramatist's mind works."

"And did you go to Birnam Wood?"

"Actually I did. And spent a night at the Birnam Trust House where dinner was served on china edged with sketches of the forest. I found that Birnam Wood is ten miles as the raven flies from Dunsinane."

"Macbeth must have had binoculars."

She was equally interested in my pursuit of the Brontes. But eventually the conversation shifted to some of our shipmates on the Queen Mary. "Did you ever follow through on your invitation from Archdeacon and Mrs. Townley to visit them in York?" she inquired.

"How did you know they invited me?" I asked, a little surprised.

"Oh, I don't know. Wasn't Lady Wylie your cabin mate? She may have mentioned it. Or maybe the archbishop himself."

"Yes, I did write them when I was in Haworth working on the Brontes. They invited me for a weekend and I accepted. Very cordial folk. Mrs. Townley was on the sidewalk—I mean pavement—to meet me when I drove up. She had Monty, the dog, tied so he wouldn't wag all over me. Somehow I hadn't expected to find an archbishop living beside a racetrack, though I don't know why not."

"You enjoyed yourself?"

"Did I ever. Marjorie, the maid, woke me at 8:30, closed the window, pushed back the drapes, left a jug of hot water and my tea tray. 'Breakfast will be shortly after nine,' she advised. 'Don't rush, love.' The Venerable was preaching at some distant parish that morning, but Mrs. Townley and I went to services at York Minster."

"How did you like the Minster?"

"It's b-i-g! Lovely in its way, but huge. Impressive. A mighty fortress, for sure. The amplifiers sent the preacher's words vibrating from corner to corner. He was half through the next sentence before the previous one stopped echoing. I found it distracting and overpowering at the same time. Apart from all its history and being an architectural wonder, I like Worcester Cathedral better."

"But you had a good time."

"Oh, splendid! The best. After tea on Sunday, the archbishop, Mrs. Townley and I drove to Crambe, where the Venerable was guest speaker at the Remembrance Day service. I thoroughly, without reservation, enjoyed that service. The little church was packed. Folks came from neighboring hamlets. Mrs. Townley and I sat in the third row behind two rows of British legionmen. Sir Roy Butcher read the lessons."

"He's a general, isn't he?"

"Yes. Yes, he is. And after the service, Sir Roy and Lady Maureen, the Venerable and Mrs. T, and I were guests of the vicar for supper. It was all so British I could not help commenting that the bacon and boiled egg pie reminded me of Sir Roger DeCoverly."

"Did that amuse them?"

"We Americans often amuse you British."

"If I remember right, Sir Roy was in India many years with the army."

"Yes, he was, and he told the most amusing as well as the most appalling stories about his experiences. But I am doing all the talking. What about you? What have you been doing since we parted?"

"I have a very busy life with Lady Baden-Powell." My questions were either too discreet or too ill-informed to ascertain anything about Miss Powell, though she talked easily about Lady Baden-Powell's continued commitment to the Boy Scouts and the Girl Guides of the world.

After dessert of ginger sponge with caramel sauce, we spent an hour in the newsreel theater. Then Miss Powell walked with me to Cavendish Square, where we parted but not before she suggested an invitation might be forthcoming from Hampton Palace.

She phoned the next morning before I had finished my toast and marmalade to confirm an invitation to lunch with Lady Baden-Powell at Hampton Court Tuesday next. Just why I was being invited I did not know. Perhaps I would learn on Tuesday. Miss Powell had merely said, "Oh, she has two or three lunches a week when she is home. Sometimes we have as many as thirty people, but I think only three or four on Tuesday. They come from everywhere—Africa, Mexico...." Umm, I thought to myself, Shall I get a long cigarette holder, wear dangling earrings, high-heeled shoes, and pose as someone? But who? Better to go in the guise of myself. Emily Dickinson's poem on the subject came to mind:

> I'm Nobody! Who are you?
> Are you—Nobody—Too?
> Then there's a pair of us!
> Don't tell! they'd advertise—you know!
>
> How dreary—to be—Somebody!
> How public—like a Frog—
> To tell one's name—the livelong June—
> To an admiring Bog!

Hampton Court was the home of reigning monarchs from the time of Henry VIII to the death of George II in 1750. Then it stood empty for almost a century until Victoria opened the State Apartments to the public. At the same time, she made nearly a thousand other rooms into apartments, which she granted to ladies of grace and favor, widows of distinguished servants of the Crown. Every succeeding monarch has followed the custom. Ladies of the palace, they call themselves. Lady Baden-Powell, chief scout of the world, is one of the ladies of grace and favor. There I went, taking the train down from London, for lunch with Miss Powell, Lady Baden-Powell, and three other guests.

I would have thought I was in a museum had a maid not met me at the door and taken my coat. As another maid ushered me down a long, wide hall, I decided I really was in a museum. Gold swords covered the walls. The late Lord Baden-Powell once said, "I have hundreds of gold swords but not one bath mat to call my own," his widow confided in the course of the afternoon's conversations. Asked once what he wanted for his birthday, he replied, "A pair of braces." Consulted about a fitting memorial to be erected to him, he decided after reflection, "The Boy Scouts will be memorial enough." His plain marker in Westminster Abbey reads simply, "Robert Baden-Powell, chief scout of the world."

From the hall I entered a large drawing room. It must have been at least thirty feet by fifty. The dimensions alone gave it a singular grandeur even without the high, frescoed ceiling. A wood fire was blazing in an intricately carved fireplace big enough for a person to stand in. An Adams, I would guess. The walls were hung with what I was to learn were the paintings of Lord Baden-Powell himself. The maid took me to my hostess, curtseyed and said, "Lady Baden-Powell, Evelyn Copeland." She in turn introduced me to Claire Laurence with whom she was talking. Miss Laurence, a member of the S.P.G. (Society for the Propagation of the Gospel) would be flying back to Malta on Friday.

"And on Sunday next," Miss Laurence exclaimed, "I am responsible for an all-day outing of I-don't-know-how-many Girl Guides. I cahn't really think how I am going to manage all that."

"And what will you be doing next Sunday?" Lady Baden-Powell asked, turning to scoop me into the conversation.

Two other guests were caught up in an animated dialogue by the fire. But where was Miss Powell? I was beginning to wonder whether she was another maid, or the cook maybe? She had said, "I have a very busy life with Lady Baden-Powell." But before I finished telling my hostess that next Sunday evening would find me in Albert Hall for a concert that would include Rachmaninoff's Piano Concerto No. 2, Miss Powell appeared. A red crepe rose replaced the New York camellia of our earlier meeting; this on the left shoulder of her bulky gray dress. She joined us for a moment and then suggested she introduce me to the other two guests, Rusty from South Africa and Mrs. Volks from Rhodesia. Shortly, lunch was announced and Lady Baden-Powell led us into the dining room, so comfortable and intimate for six that I wondered where she entertains parties of thirty.

Luncheon conversation roamed from gardening to the British economy (Times have been difficult since the war. Lady B-P has had to let her gardener go. She is managing now with two maids, cook, and chauffeur) to music (Whether Mrs. Volks prefers Albert Hall to the Royal Festival depends upon who is conducting. She'd prefer Sir Thomas Beecham over Cyril Smith whichever hall he was in.). Everyone except me was involved one way or another with the Girl Guides. That topic ran throughout the afternoon. But we also touched upon the war, which everyone is still trying to get beyond. Apropos of the tinned black currants served for dessert, Miss Powell recalled a message she received during the war, "Have ninety tons of plums. Can you help us tin?" She could. More war stories followed.

Since I had been doing some work on Shakespeare, Lady Baden-Powell thought I would be interested to know that her bedroom was Shakespeare's Green Room when he lived at Hampton Court Palace. And no, she would not mind at all if I took pictures. Perhaps I would like to see the Great Hall where his plays were performed for Queen Elizabeth, the Earl of Essex, and their ilk? The Great Hall is not part of her grace and favor apartment, but Miss Powell's bedroom on the floor above opens into the minstrels' balcony of the Great Hall. I was promised a tour later.

After lunch the guests did not leave, but they scattered. My hostess wanted to show me her roof garden with its skyline of higgledy-piggledy chimney pots. On our way, she especially pointed out a bench that was a gift from Koshkonong, Missouri, U.S.A. Our tour also included her two-room annex with linen paneling and Tudor ceilings. To get a sense of the size of the annex, picture four hundred and fifty American Girl Guides bedded down here at one time. What a slumber party! Rusty, one of our luncheon companions, ran this annex during the war, not for American Girl Guides, but for whoever needed a refuge.

Before we reached the roof garden, Lady B-P dropped me off in a room with shelves and shelves of scrapbooks, suggesting I might like to browse through America 1953-54, a record of her visit the previous year to fifty-seven American cities. However, before I finished looking through that scrapbook, Miss Powell arrived to take me on a tour of the palace.

We found Lady Twining feeding ducks beside the palace pool. After a short chat, we went on to the Great Hall where some of Shakespeare's plays were originally performed. That was almost as heady as visiting the site of the Globe Theatre in London. And much more exclusive. Next we toured the State Apartments, where I walked in the footsteps of plump old Henry VIII himself. In the Apartments Museum I saw paintings, tapestries, and Queen Mary's (of William and Mary) delft among other treasures. One painting, Arabella Stewart, is said to have been originally titled Queen Elizabeth in Fancy Dress, but Elizabeth objected, saying she looked pregnant. So the painting was retouched and renamed. Makes me wonder who Mona Lisa was originally.

I, with the other guests, returned from our various pursuits of the afternoon to the drawing room for tea at four. The conversation, as lively and diverse as before, turned eventually to three writers who are simultaneously working on biographies of Lord Baden-Powell "without consulting me, his diaries, or his scrapbooks," sniffed Lady Baden-Powell.

After tea I returned to London with Mrs. Volks on the five o'clock train. The next day I sent flowers. It seemed the thing to do. I also wrote a Collins (a bread and butter letter so named for the impeccable thank-you notes Mr. Collins wrote in Jane Austin's Pride and Prejudice) to both Lady Baden-Powell and Miss Powell. I was still not sure what role Miss Powell plays. Public relations? Palace tour guide? Social secretary? Companion? Sister-in-law? All of the above?

My days continued to be full. Helen Layton came up again from Oxford. She had invited me to join her and Grace Weinberg for lunch, and when she learned her train was going to be early, phoned to suggest I meet her at the Royal Academy to visit the Eighteenth Century Masters Exhibit. The reviews had been superlative. We had only time to dip into two rooms: some Canalettos (1697-1768), a few Hogarths (1697-1764) and several Reynolds (1723-1792). I was a little disappointed to have found only one of my favorite Fragonards before we had to leave to meet Grace at the National Book League on Albemarle Street. But I could get to that on my own any day while the exhibit lasted. The Book League was just the sort of cultured spot Helen knows about for lunch.

Grace is an ardent admirer of Norway. She heartily endorsed my impulse to strike out on my own to visit there. With the help of the Norwegian Travel Bureau in Trafalgar Square, I should have no problems, she assured me, with either language or hospitality. She will introduce me to the Anglo-Norwegian attaché if I like and will invite me to the Anglo-Norwegian club when it meets.

I was eager to go to the Lofoten Islands off the coast of Norway in the North Sea, the home of Rolvaag, author of Giants in the Earth. It is the story of nineteenth-century immigrants in South Dakota. I have followed their route in the States across the plains to their sod huts. Next I would like to see the lonely islands from which those seafarers came.

After lunch Helen and Grace left to see Peggy Ashcroft in Hedda Gabler, and I made my way to the British Museum for the three o'clock lecture on the Sutton Hoo Ship Burial. In Bay X of the King Edward VIII Gallery for a spell-binding hour and a half, a lecturer told our small group the story behind the exhibits: silver bowls and spoons, gold jewelry, a scepter whetstone, a pattern-welded sword set with garnets. One helmet was pieced together from over a thousand bits, the work of six months. The lecturer pointed out the uses and intricacies of a drinking horn, a small quadrangle harp, hanging bowls, and a reconstructed shield. This was a royal commemorative burial of A.D. 650-70. The burial, as far as scholars can determine, probably honored King Anna or his brother King Aethelhere. Interestingly, no body accompanied the commemorative articles.

About two weeks after my lunch with Lady Baden-Powell came another invitation from Miss Powell for "a buffet for three or four." I RSVPed my acceptance and on February 25 arrived at Hampton Court Palace to find more like twenty-three or -four buzzing in small groups in the drawing room. I recognized Rusty from the previous luncheon and spotted Lady Baden-Powell in an animated conversation with a courtly looking, bewhiskered gentleman. The rest were strangers to me. When the buffet arrived, our hostess rang a little oriental bell and said, "Help yourselves and find a place around a table to continue your chatter." We gathered in fours and fives around little tables that were part of the drawing room décor—carved ivory here, polished ebony there. I found my way to one inlaid with chards of jade. They represented some of the countries where Lord Baden-Powell had established the Boy Scouts. We sat on little chairs and campstools that had been placed around them and nibbled goodies from the buffet—asparagus sandwiches, stuffed eggs, meat patties—and talked. I learned I was partaking in a Thinking Day.

All over the world this week Girl Guides are celebrating Thinking Day. The idea originated in 1932 at a world conference of Girl Guides. The event always occurs during the third week of February to coincide with Lady Baden-Powell's birthday. Girl Guides think of what the organization stands for and ways to improve their work, spirit, and attitude. In the course of the week over four hundred and fifty groups from every possible nook on the globe send Lady Baden-Powell, their chief, birthday cards and messages.

Periodically the chief, who sat in a stuffed chair at the edge of one of the little tables, rang her tiny bell and called out, "Let's change places." Then everyone, except our hostess, milled around and found a new set of companions. Though this shift did interrupt some good conversations it did provide an opportunity to revisit the buffet and to meet eventually all of the guests. In one segment I met a woman who had started her Girl Guide work in Nigeria but was now working with scouts in a leper colony in Baazudaland. "Our Africa," the chief sighed fondly. She pointed out a South African stool in the drawing room. "The size of the stool indicates one's prestige," she explained. Then with a twinkle she added, "You can see our stools are very small."

Someone asked about a camel saddle near a Chinese chest. "Oh that," she said. "The most uncomfortable thing imaginable. Don't ever try to ride a camel. But the apartment is strewn with saddles. You'll see them everywhere, a popular gift to Lord Robert."

When the next time came to change places, she said to me, "Go talk with the lady in the brown suit. I don't know her name, but she is fascinating."

The lady in the brown suit was Mrs. Tebbs from Chestfield near Canterbury. She was a graduate of Cambridge, where she had majored in (or read as the British say) English literature and showed more than a casual interest in my literary tour of Great Britain. We talked of the Brontes and the Lake poets. And which Hardy novel was our favorite. She favored Tess of the D'Ubervilles. I, having come so recently from tramping Egdon Heath, thought Return of the Native was mine.

"What about Blackmore's Lorna Doone?" she asked. "Are you going to Exmoor?"

"I'd like to because I understand it is so beautiful, but since we do not read Lorna Doone in my classes back home, it may have to wait for my next visit."

"Have you been to Canterbury yet?" she asked.

"Not yet. I'm saving that for spring."

"Oh," she flashed back quick as a lick, "you mean

Whan that Aprille with his shoures soote
the droughte of March hath perced to the roote...
than longen folk to goon on pilgrimages?"

Her middle English so surprised me that I could scarcely stutter,

"And palmers for to saken strange strondes,
to ferne halwes, kouthe in sondre londes."

But she understood: "Yes, when April comes, I, too, like Chaucer's pilgrims, will wend my way to Canterbury."

"And when you do, you must come and have lunch with me."

"And," said Mr. Bickersteth, who had not had much to say up to that point, "you must let me show you around the cathedral. I will show you the very spot where the king's men murdered Thomas à Becket. Do your students in America know Becket's story?"

"Some of them do. My seniors read selections from Chaucer's Canterbury Tales and also T.S. Eliot's Murder in the Cathedral."

"Good, good," he nodded approvingly.

Mr. Bickersteth, I learned, lives almost in the shadow of the cathedral, and obviously takes a great personal interest in the edifice. But before we could pursue this promising discussion further, our hostess rang her bell and announced, "Now that you seem to have abandoned the buffet, I'd like to ask all of you who are connected with the Guides to tell us how you first became interested and where you work now."

The first to speak up was an American woman who had been working with the Guides in Heidelberg for three years. She was at the moment on a week's leave in London. "But this leave is no rest," she gasped. "We are on an organized tour. They had us up at dawn to visit the Caledonian Market this morning." Mrs. Robie, also an American, works with Girl Guides in thirty-six U.S. Army camps all over Europe. Sir Frank (Somebody) told the story of a stuttering Boy Scout who for his good deed sat out two dances with a lonely lady. At that point Miss Powell sought me out, the first opportunity we had had to speak since I arrived.

"You don't have to listen to all this scout talk," she whispered. "Come with me." Once out of the room, she said, "Let's get a little breath of fresh air, stroll around the pool, and then I will give you a tour of Lady Baden-Powell's annex. I believe she pointed it out when you were here before, but it deserves a closer look."

When we returned to the others about an hour later, some of the guests were already leaving. Mrs. Tebbs gave me her phone number and said, "Be sure to call when you come to Canterbury. I mean it."

"And don't let anyone but me give you a tour of the cathedral," Mr. Bickersteth added. He was leaving with Mrs. Tebbs, both taking the train back to Canterbury. He handed me his card: J. Burgon Bickersteth, Esq., 4 Burgate House, Burgate, Canterbury.

As I said goodbye to Mr. Monier-Williams, who was hosting for Lady Baden-Powell, he said, "You must come to see our bombed-site garden in June."

"But don't wait until then," his wife, standing beside him, added. "I will ring you up some day soon."

True to her word, one morning about a fortnight later as I was licking up the last of my toast and marmalade, she rang to ask whether I could drop in at six that evening, Cheyne Court, Chelsea Embankment. I could. I did. During tea she reminded me to come back in June to see how they and their neighbors had beautified a block of the Chelsea Embankment that had been left an ugly rubble after the war.

"It has had its share of publicity," Mr. Monier-Williams remarked modestly. "The Queen Mother visited it last year and had her picture taken in it."

"And it has been the subject of a radio broadcast in Australia," his wife added. I promised to return in June.

I don't know exactly how the Monier-Williams fit into the Hampton Court Palace puzzle. Lady Baden-Powell has referred to her as her sister-in-law, and my Miss Powell, among all her other ambassadorship activities, takes care of his mother, aged eighty-five, who also lives at Hampton Court. All I really know is that they are a gracious couple, living in luxurious quarters in Chelsea with their nine-year-old cat, Timothy.

March was drawing to a close. Days were getting longer. A recent visit to the Ideal Home Exhibition at Olympia, sponsored by the Daily Mail, concluded with "The Garden of Music, the Oasis You are Seeking." What roses! What tulips! Carnations, daffodils, magnolias, snowdrops! Anemones, pools, streams, willow trees, lush green grass!

Ken Phelps reminded me we must

> Go down to Kew in lilac time, in lilac time,
> Go down to Kew in lilac time (it isn't far from London).

I couldn't wait for lilacs, but Ken and I did go down to Kew Gardens. Spring was everywhere. It was time for me to set out for Canterbury in the footsteps of Chaucer's pilgrims.

Taking advantage of the opportunities that had opened at Lady Baden-Powell's luncheon, I phoned Mr. Bickersteth. He remembered me and suggested we meet at the cathedral at two o'clock Tuesday week. Next I phoned Mrs. Tebbs, the guest who had quoted Chaucer in Middle English.

"Yes, yes, my dear. I've been anticipating your call. When are you coming to Canterbury?"

"Next week."

"Will you be able to come to lunch with me on Wednesday?"

"I'd love to."

"Good. Come promptly at twelve because I have a meeting at three." She gave directions for getting to her in Chestfield, near Canterbury.

Committed now to leaving London, I scurried about my current work on Dickens at the London Library and photographing places associated with him in London. In addition I had one more social invitation to enjoy.

I met Mrs. Monier-Willams in Chelsea one afternoon and walked with her past their famous bombed-site embankment to Crosby Hall. The gardens were blanketed with crocuses, anemones, and snowdrops.

Bombed site garden

"How can these gardens be any more beautiful in June than they are now?" I exclaimed.

"Just wait and see," she said. "You will come back, won't you?"

"I give my word."

That particular afternoon we were on our way to meet Dr. Broom at Crosby Hall, the only medieval hall still standing in London. It was moved to its present site from Bishop's Gate about 1910 and was miraculously spared—except for glass and front doors—when so many buildings were bombed right up to it in the recent war. Dr. Broom was host for tea in the gallery of the hall. He had also invited Miss Kemble, a student of Byron from California, whom I had not met before. Nor had I met Dr. Broom until that afternoon, just another bit of Miss Powell's sleight of hand.

"One lump or two?" he inquired, playing Mother.

Over the click of teaspoons on delicate Lemoge and between bites of dainty pastries, the discussion roamed like Childe Harold all over the face of English literature as well as the pilgrimages of his two American guests. The sun was setting as we made our farewells. In parting, Dr. Broom reminded us we were looking out at the view that inspired many of Turner's sunsets.

I could not leave London, however, without thanking Miss Powell once more for all the doors she had opened, so many pleasures, so much information for which she had been directly or indirectly responsible. I suggested lunch in the city. "But, my dear, you must see the crocuses at Hampton Court," she pleaded. So, since my car was out of winter storage, I proposed picking her up and driving into the country.

At Hampton Court crocuses of every color dotted the lawns like colored hailstones from a summer shower. I photographed crocuses en masse, crocuses with ducks, crocuses with Miss Lynette Powell in her blue New York hat with a red feather and her bright, straw basket from Pitcairn Island, a basket Lady Baden-Powell had brought from one of her Girl Guide excursions.

We stopped briefly in Kingston for Miss Powell to buy nightgown material and hair tonic. Then on to Esher through Wesley to Guilford.

Stretches of heath separated the villages with their little front-door gardens already vibrant in spring colors. Guilford is an attractive old town with an ancient boys' grammar school, a not so ancient flint church, and half-timbered shops. The High runs down to Astolat Café, where we had a leisurely lunch. Guilford is the legendary site of King Arthur's Astolat. In Alfred Lord Tennyson's Idylls of the King

> Elaine the Fair,
> Elaine the Lovable,
> Elaine, the Lily Maid of Astolat,
> high in her tower to the east,
> guarded the sacred shield of Launcelot.

There in the Astolat Café Miss Powell and I chatted the afternoon away. She is a dear little enigmatic person. I have called her a hummingbird, but sometimes she sits so quietly I wonder whether blue heron might be more appropriate. Sometimes she seems a waif with her tousled hair and outsized cardigans, with her paper flowers on lapels or bright feathers in her hats. But the store of anecdotes and personages she carries around in that head both amaze and amuse. In Portugal she once wanted to ask for "food to fatten the turkeys," but she confused the word for turkey with the one for prostitute.

She told me of an Englishman who in giving an address to a Chezkoslovian audience started in the native tongue with "Ladies and gentlemen," words he had studied carefully in railroad stations. He did not know why the audience was convulsed to be greeted, "Ladies toilets and gentlemen's conveniences."

She peppered our lunch of lamb cutlets, peas and carrots, French rolls, and meringues with a string of such gems until the conversation turned to what I had been doing.

"What literary giants have you been pursuing since last we met?" she queried.

"Dickens, mostly. A little Jane Austen. Browning, incidentally. I lunched one day at the Cheshire Cheese and thought of Johnson. But mostly Dickens."

"You've visited the Old Curiosity Shop?"

"Yes, several times actually...and photographed it."

"Where else have you sought Dickens out?"

"I found Coram's Field on the site of the old Founding Hospital in the Holburn area."

"Isn't that where Handel was so impressed in the quaintly dressed children?"

"Yes, and Hogarth, too, as well as Dickens. Tattycoram was a foundling in Little Dorrit. The Hospital Office Building has many mementoes of those days. I even saw Tattycoram out there just a few days ago. Playing soccer. He couldn't have been more than six or seven, in white shorts, red top, black-and-white striped socks, and soccer boots. He seemed lame until he ran. Then how he charged. In moments between plays he wiped his grimy hands on the hip pockets of his white shorts. He was darling."

"And where else?"

"Oh, I find Dickens everywhere. I've been to Saint Luke's Parish in Chelsea where he was married and to Devonshire Terrace at the north end of Marlebone High, which was his home at one time. It's a narrow little street, crowded the morning I was there with milkmen's vans and British railway carts. Very picturesque. Quite a contrast to Harley Street with its long rows of Regency balconies and beautifully polished doors with huge knockers. I took lots of pictures of both streets. But many places associated with him, or his characters, no longer exist."

"Such as?"

"Well, Barnard's Inn where Pip in Great Expectations lived when he came to London. The site is now marked 'Bomb Site Car Park.' And I couldn't find the churchyard where Jerry Cruncher used to go fishing. Nearby, though, was a skeleton of a church, a shell with no roof. On the boards was a sign, 'Presbyterian Church. Services as usual.'"

"Yes, we haven't recovered from the war by any means," she said rather meditatively.

"I found Buckingham Street where Dickens took rooms when he first came to London, but his pudding shops were all gone."

"Where do you go next?"

"To Canterbury."

"And Burgon Bickersteth and Mrs. Tebbs."

"Yes, thanks to you."

"And Lady Baden-Powell. Mrs. Monier-Williams and Mrs. Tebbs studied together at Cambridge years ago."

I tried to thank Miss Powell for all she had done to enrich my London experience, but she dismissed it as just another day in the life of Lady Baden-Powell.

I did not see Miss Powell again until August. Mrs. Monier-Williams had invited me for dinner prior to my departure for home. Miss Powell, returning from a holiday in Sussex, was spending a few days with her. We all walked once more to the bombed-site garden before tea. I had returned in June as promised to see the roses and admitted the show was worth a special trip from anywhere. After tea Mrs. Monier-Williams left Miss Powell and me to have a good natter while she tended to dinner.

At dinner the conversation turned to remembrances of childhood. Childhood? Yes, Miss Powell must once have been a child. She remembered wondering, "How does one covet a neighbor's house if covet is a big white sheet?"

"Whom did Cain and Abel marry?"

"Grasshoppers," her nanny told her.

"Who was my mummy when my mummy was a little girl?"

When asked as a child where she might find elephants, she did not know why grownups laughed at her reply that she wouldn't expect to find them anywhere because they don't get lost.

A lopsided moon hung over the London skyline when we parted late that evening. I would be boarding the Queen Elizabeth for home in a few days. My host was driving me back to my room tonight. Miss Powell watched from the front steps as he and I went down the walk to his car. Who is this wisp of a remarkable woman—really? I wondered, as I returned her goodbye wave.

Tea with the Children

(diary excerpt)
Oxford
March 20, 1955

You can read about them in Alice in Wonderland and numerous other places, but English children at Sunday afternoon tea must be seen to be thoroughly believed. I have had Sunday tea with Helen Layton's Timothy, age fourteen, but Lady Wylie's three grandchildren and their two guests are in the eight-to-ten age bracket.

"We went to New Zealand this afternoon, Gran," one announced, "but some monsters drove us away." New Zealand is a wooded area near Wooton Ridge; the monsters were older boys.

"But has anyone here ever really been to New Zealand?" eight-year-old Roger asked.

"I have," said his sister.

"Really?" another child asked.

"Well, Australia...that's almost New Zealand."

"It is not," cousin Keith blinked authoritatively.

There followed a discussion of geography that taxed my vague notions of the spatial relationships of New Zealand, Khartoun, Cyprus, and other places that one or another of the youngsters had visited or lived in. Their friend Charles, with a very black eye earned at the end of a cricket bat, had lived in Cyprus. Susan and Roger's parents live in Khartoon. Susan was born in Australia. Keith's father is just a Cambridge professor. Uncle Francis, head of dayboys at Dragon, inquired about recent exams. Roger had twenty-eight out of thirty right in Latin.

"Susan? Any tests?"

"I got an F for failure, but I had more right than wrong," she explained.

"Did anyone have more wrong than right?" her brother wanted to know.

"Yes, two."

"Oh, well, you weren't the worst."

Easter holidays are approaching and the youngsters speculated on how early they could leave school. Charles's comment was lost to me in the din, but I loved Roger's "But my dear boy, how can we breakfast at 7:15 if we sleep until 7:30?"

All this time Granny's tea was disappearing with great rapidity equaled only by meticulous propriety. Once, just once, Susan missed her cue to pass Ruth's cup to Granny for more tea, and once Keith was dissolved in chagrin when he realized he had accepted a piece of cake while there was still an end of chocolate biscuit on his plate. Should he return the cake? Crimson to his ear tips, he looked beseechingly at Uncle Francis.

"Eat it up, chap," Uncle Francis said consolingly. "Just pay more attention next time."

Tea progressed and so did the chatter, but Emily Post could have found little fault with these little ones. Never an elbow on the table, never a word with the mouth full despite the enthusiasm.

After tea Uncle Francis stowed them into his Black Maria for delivery at their respective boarding schools but not until each one, clutching a bag of goodies from Gram, had shaken hands with me in the drawing room and said a proper thank you to Gram for the pleasant day.

A Toast to the Soroptimists

(diary excerpt)
Nuneaton, Warwickshire
April 28, 1955

I have lost track—actually I never had a count—of the number of British churches I have visited, but never have I done one so thoroughly as the Nuneaton Parish Church of St. Nichols today. I have been inside the pipe organ works, up a straight, narrow ladder on a diversion from the tower stairs to observe the workings of the clock, and even walked the planks between the tops of the eight great bells. This morning's paper pictured Queen Elizabeth standing over the steward's box at the Newmarket races yesterday. The headline pointed out that no guardrail separated the queen from the melee below. I am not trying to compete with Her Majesty for precariousness of position, but I was inspired by that picture when my little sexton guide stepped out on a narrow plank with no more than a "mind your step" to me. I saw the ropes tied securely around the huge wheel that turns each bell. I pulled the rope (a bit), examined the hammer, and tapped the bells for tone and resonance. In this new £8,000 organ he did not want me to miss a thing. He extracted a few tiny pipes for me to blow through, and since the organist was still playing, he could also point out how the bellows worked.

Then in the bell room under the bells, where the eight ropes dangle—each bound in its red, white, and blue covering—the sexton showed me a boxful of old bells of all sizes and let me try them. I wanted to stay and pick out at least one tune—"Jingle Bells," maybe—but he had already given me over an hour of his time, and the pile of fuzz and dust he had been sweeping up when I walked in waited in front of the altar with the dustpan beside it.

I had approached this wood and stone church shortly after lunch. Daffodils brightened my approach. Someone was playing the organ. The sexton had welcomed me with a firm handshake and invited me to look at the pictures in the vestry. "Is your vestry like this?" he queried. He took the eighteenth-century communion service from the safe, wanting me to handle it, lift and examine each piece. "What is your church silver like?" he wanted to know. Then followed the tour. At the end of all that he looked me straight in the eye and asked, "What do you think?" I responded enthusiastically and thanked him for all the time he had given me. It was time, however, to start giving some thought to the toast I was to propose at the meeting of the Soroptimists tomorrow evening,

Nuneaton, Warwickshire
April 29, 1955

The King's Head Inn, Free House, serves a mighty delicious shredded cheese and raw onion sandwich with a "my dear"-ing waiter, a retired navy captain from an aircraft carrier. He knows every inch of this "dear little island," he told me and could recommend every stately house on it for me to visit—all with dear little gardens. As he talked, I was conjuring up in my mind some appropriate remarks to make this evening at the Coventry Soroptimists annual meeting. Last November at the George Eliot banquet Alice Lynes had asked me to return this spring to reply to the toast to the guests at Coventry's annual meeting. I stalled, but eventually succumbed, bowing to the philosophy that something can be learned from every experience. Now the night had arrived and I was sitting at the head table.

A Mr. Iliffe was proposing a toast to the guests. Apropos of the origin of the Soroptimists organization, he remarked that Americans claimed it had started there but "Americans never tell the truth, so we won't count what they say." Encouraged by the mild titter this brought from the audience, he went on to say a few more belittling things about Americans, each time getting a little more laughter. Apparently he had not read the program and seen that an American was going to reply to him. It was equally apparent that many at the tables were aware of my presence.

A little later when the toastmaster pounded his gavel and prayed silence for Miss Evelyn Copeland of Connecticut, USA, Madame President, sitting next to me, leaned over and said, "Give it to him."

I began: "Madame President, Mr. Deputy Mayor, My Lord Bishop, ladies and gentlemen, this is the first time I have ever spoken in public in Great Britain and until a few minutes ago I felt as Peter Rabbit did in Mr. McGregor's garden 'breathless and trembling with fright,' but Mr. Iliffe has put me at ease with his assurance that you need pay no attention to what I say because there will no truth in it. (Applause) But I am glad to have an opportunity to say thank you not only as a guest at this elegant banquet but as a guest in Great Britain. Alice Duer Miller, a compatriot of mine, wrote some fifteen years ago:

"I have loved England dearly and deeply
since that first morning, shining and pure,
the White Cliffs of Dover I saw rising steeply
out of the sea that once made her secure.

"My first glimpse of those cliffs came only two months ago, but like Alice Duer Miller I have loved England since that morning nearly two years ago when the Brittanic nosed her way up the Mersey through a misty sunrise to dock in Liverpool Harbor. I speak for all the guests here tonight as well as for my own experiences over recent months when I say thank you for your unfailing hospitality."

The Worthingtons

THE YEAR WAS 1983. I had recently lost a close friend to colon cancer and was seeking solace in a sentimental journey to Great Britain. Among the friends I looked forward to visiting were the Worthingtons, two sisters and their brother Michael. Unhampered by family except for each other, since none of them had ever married, they were free to pursue their busy lives at will. I had always found these lives unusually vibrant, intellectually motivated, and refreshingly challenging.

I had known Dorothy for more than twenty-five years, from the time she came from Wales as an exchange teacher of English to Norwalk High School in Norwalk, Connecticut. I was teaching at the time in nearby Fairfield and because a colleague and I had recently spent a summer in Stratford-upon-Avon, the Exchange Program Committee asked us to meet and entertain her one weekend soon after her arrival. Without further formalities we named ourselves her official guides to New England. With the arrival of winter we introduced her to skiing. She sampled Maine lobster and Boston baked beans with brown bread. She ate peach fritters with my family on Good Friday, as was our tradition. She journeyed to Belfast, Maine, with Winnie during spring vacation, and went sledding with our friends in Peterborough, New Hampshire. When school closed in June, she traveled with Winnie and me to an English conference in Chicago. From there some of her Norwalk colleagues took over her transcontinental tour.

Dorothy's view of America through fresh eyes, her reactions candidly expressed, and her insatiable curiosity about all things large and small made her a prized guest wherever she went and a welcome companion even if she did not go anywhere. Why, she wondered, that first afternoon on skis, are American children's cheeks so pale? Are they unused to exercise? Or, as we finally concluded, not living in an island country, do American children tend to have less rosy cheeks than their counterparts in Britain? Or, "Your breakfast bread tastes sweet to me. Is this general throughout American bakeries? And do you sweeten your own homemade breads?" "Does hearing Macbeth in an American accent do an injustice to Shakespeare?" "Why do you put ice in your drinking water? It makes my teeth shudder." These were observations, not complaints. She tended to open our eyes to ourselves. Her comments rarely dead-ended. Dorothy was above all else a good conversationalist, conversing being an art, it seems to me, more praised than practiced in twentieth century America.

In the intervening years, Dorothy and I have frequently visited back and forth across the ocean. This was my fourth or fifth (I have lost track) trip to the Worthingtons' home in Llanidloes, Wales, not counting the times I have met Dorothy or Michael more briefly in London. On this occasion I met Michael at his flat in Belgrave Mansions, the St. John's Woods area of London. Dorothy, who had been shopping in London, joined us there, and we were soon on our way by motorcar to Llanidloes. For the next four hours heavy mists obscured most of the magnificent views Dorothy and Mike assured me were out there. We did, however, get glimpses of attractive towns, had a peek at Burford from the bypass and actually took a teeny detour around the open-market hall in Pembridge, a town of half-timbered cottages and inns jumbled around a medieval market place. Its rambling New Inn dates back to 1311.

As we approached Llanidloes, I saw a sign pointing a divergence to Hope Under Dinmor and commented, "I wonder who Dinmor is."

"I wonder who Hope is," Dorothy countered. Nearby was the hamlet of Lower Hope, Mike told me, and we speculated as to how many more Hopes were nearby and which one any one of us would prefer to have for an address.

Marjory was standing in the doorway to greet us when we reached their home, Hafod (meaning summer dwelling), Garden Suburb. After tea and much talk, she asked whether I would like faggots for supper. From my reading of Thomas Hardy's Return of the Native I was acquainted with the term faggots. After Clym Yeobright in that novel became blind, he gathered faggots for a livelihood, sticks of gorse or furze that grow on the heath. They are bundled and used for brooms or burned for heat. Surely this was not what Marjory meant to serve for supper. Noting my moment of perplexity, Mike clarified the term for me, "Faggots are made of minced pig's liver, bread crumbs, onions, and sage rolled into balls and cooked in the oven in water. It's my favorite dish." And I did indeed have faggots and peas for supper.

The next morning Dorothy and I walked into town through drizzle and mist, but we were properly done up in our macs, each carrying a red umbrella should the drizzle turn to rain. The walk took us past The Hollies, Mike's birthplace, as he was fond of pointing out. My previous visits had always been to The Hollies, a charming four-hundred-year-old residence. My family's hundred-and-fifty-year-old farm was modern in comparison. Dorothy's parents, who were both living when I first visited, had since died. What wonderful, witty, storytelling folk they were. I miss them.

On we went into town by way of the Old Market Hall, which also dates from the sixteenth century. It is the only timber-framed market hall that survives today in Wales. Its weathervane dates from 1738. We crossed the bridge that spans the confluence of the Severn and Clywedog rivers, and continued along the river path up to the Welsh parish church of St. Idloes, which started as a cell when Christianity first came to Wales. A Mrs. Stevens, who was polishing the brass and arranging the flowers for tomorrow, turned the lights on, the better to admire the mammoth pillars and the angels interspersed around the ceiling.

From there we strolled back to the Old Market Hall and Great Oak Street with its New (Jacobian) Market Hall, a philanthropic donation to the town by Lord Davies in 1908. Laura Ashley, who has materials shops all over the world, is a native of Wales. Dorothy and I visited one of her stores in Toronto last October. This morning we stopped in at one of her original shops. At Black Weavers, another weaving shop, I met the chief weaver and owner (with her Irish husband). She is from Virginia, USA.

It was market day with barrows and lorries set up along Great Oak. Dorothy and I browsed. I bought three small boxes at an Indian stall that was redolent with incense. We had elevensies in the Great Oak Café and later wandered through the New Market Hall with its cheeses, breads, gorgeous thick knit sweaters, and countless trinkets. It was a real undercover market, undercover meaning roofed over but open to the street.

After a brief stop at the dispensary where Marjorie works, and where I met the receptionist and "the old doc," Dorothy decided we did have time to "pop into" Hafren Furnishers. Hafren is Welsh for seven. She had pointed it out to me as we walked into town, explaining that it is the largest distributors of furniture in Great Britain and that folks come from as far as Edinburgh to shop because the selections are so extensive. Privately, viewing it from across the street, I thought it looked like a second-hand store for wicker furniture, but since we had time, I was willing to take a look. And, oh, my goodness! All I could say was, "Did you ever!" as Dorothy lead me back, back, back (almost to the next village) and then started returning on an upper level. She said we did not have time for the lower level, for it would never do to be late for Mike's dinner. I had no idea of buying anything as we crowded by living room suites (some even suspended at eye-level over those on the floor), rows and rows of beds, dining room tables in every possible size, sewing tables, coffee tables, complete kitchens…until we turned a corner and I spied on the wall eight different thimble display cases. Michael groaned when we reached home and Dorothy told him she had given me a tour of Hafren Furnishers, but he was incredulous when I said I had bought something, a thimble display case. Not that I have any thimbles, but I have a friend who collects miniatures. I think the display case is unique as travel gifts go.

Dorothy and I reached Hafod just before one o'clock to find Michael putting the finishing touches on a sumptuous steak-and-kidney pie. Green peas, boiled potatoes and bubbly, homemade apple cider (apple champagne) completed the dinner, topped off, of course, with a sweet—this time, pineapple pudding.

After dinner off we went, Michael driving, to see the incredible hills and vales of central Wales. Though this was not the setting, I was reminded of How Green Was My Valley and could picture Katherine Hepburn, hair flying, riding her bicycle against the background of green pastures and grazing sheep. We stopped at the ruins of an old lead mining camp with a miners' bridge on the outskirts of Llanidloes. Of course I took pictures, and I took more pictures at the Clywedog Dam and later, as we drove on, of the lake the dam creates. The valleys and hills cry out to be photographed, but I finally put my camera away and abandoned myself to enjoying the splendor. Mike wanted me to see the waterfall at Dylife, Cwn Pennant Valley, even though because of the dry summer the water was not falling. Cwn means valley. If I have the name right, it appears to me to be redundant, but I make no claims when it comes to coping with the Welsh language. We poked around Machynlleth (don't ask me to pronounce it) and did a little shopping.

Thanks to Mike and Dorothy, my Welsh vocabulary grew a little that afternoon. To wit:

gwyddrug . . . . .mound or wooded knoll
llwm . . . . .bared or exposed
maes . . . . .open field or plain
llethr . . . . .slope
coch . . . . .red
llan . . . . .church

Llanidloes (Church of Idloes) was only a church until in 1280 it received a market charter from the king. Its greatest prosperity came from weaving during the first half of the nineteenth century. Judging from the sheep I see everywhere I go in Wales, both in the fields and in the roads, I think it must still be prosperous. Royalty itself dines on Welsh lamb, as I shall myself tomorrow evening, Dorothy tells me. In fact, the butcher shop proudly displays the Royal Crest proclaiming that the royal family bought lamb in Llanidloes.

Unless one is born to the Welsh tongue, speaking it should be left to the natives. "A foreign tongue just cannot cope with it," Dorothy told me when I first met her and thought perhaps I could learn to pronounce Llanidloes as she does. In the course of the afternoon, I added other words to my journal if not my speaking vocabulary:

ogof . . . . .cave
gorffwyofa . . . .resting place
ystrad . . . . .valley
rhyd . . . . .ford
mynydd . . . . .mountain or moorland
rhaeadr . . . . . . .waterfall

ffridd . . . . .wood or mountain

Our afternoon jaunt took us finally through Commins Coch, reminding Michael that he once had a kitten named Commins Coch because someone from there gave it to him. Though he scarcely remembers the cat, his mother, he told me, never forgot it.

Home with Marjorie in the evening we listened to (and watched) Verdi's Ernani on BBC. Later that evening in the lull that followed our discussion of the opera and we had moved on somehow to holidays, Mike said, "Eve' lyn, why don't you join Dor, Mar, and me next week in our holiday to Bruges?"

"Well, why not?" I said hesitantly. "Let me think about it a minute."

"Minute's up," Dorothy said.

Without much further discussion we seemed to agree we would return to London on Monday, make arrangements for a four-day holiday in Bruges on Tuesday and spend the rest of the week abroad. I had been in Belgium on an earlier trip to Europe, visiting a friend in Antwerp, but never to Bruges. This would be a first and I was a little bit excited not only by the prospect but the spontaneity of the whole project.

Only one thing was written in stone on Sunday morning: dinner would be at 12:30 P.M. I was on my own until then, and so I decided to stroll back to town, camera in hand. Eavesdropping as folks were leaving chapel, I heard considerable Welsh mixed in with English. I took pictures chiefly of the Old Market Hall and people coming and going from the one store that sells Sunday papers along with milk and other miscellany. The milk is sold in pint glass bottles beside the door without refrigeration. I wish I had dared to snap a picture of the man who was trying to cope with five pint bottles and the Sunday paper. Groceries are not bagged in Great Britain unless you bring your own bag, and this chap did not have a bag.

Marjorie had shared with me earlier a little tidbit about the man who owns the paper store. He has the concession to sell Sunday papers through his divorce settlement. He and his wife used to sell papers seven days a week. Since their divorce, she sells the dailies in her store and he sells the Sundays in his store.

Dorothy, Marjorie, and Michael are not only walking histories of Wales but also encyclopedias of who is who in the literary world. I never know where a small item may lead. For instance, today's paper had a review of Elizabeth Longford's Elizabeth R: A Biography. The review itself was of only passing interest but served as a springboard into the intrigues in the life of Elizabeth Langford's daughter, Antonia Frazier.

The centerpiece of the meal I returned to from my Sunday morning walk (and which was served precisely at 12:30 P.M.) was the roast chicken Marjorie and Michael had stuffed so lovingly the night before. And surely more than two hands had been involved in preparing the boiled potatoes, the brightest orange carrots I have ever seen, the cauliflower, bread sauce, chicken gravy, and pudding that filled out the meal. It is common knowledge that the Welsh have beautiful singing voices. Anyone who visits the Worthingtons will soon learn that their culinary skills are equally outstanding.

After Sunday dinner I had a choice of visiting Aberystwyth and the university or driving to the desert and the Birmingham reservoirs. I had seen the university at Aberystwyth on a previous visit, an impressive campus that looks down upon the Irish Sea with its pounding waves and long sandy beach. I recalled how eager I was for Dorothy to see Long Island Sound when she first came to Connecticut...proud that I lived only half a mile from it. Residents on Rowland Road had free access to the beach, where we frequently swam in the summer. I realized later when I saw Aberystwyth the first time that my twenty feet of private access to Long Island Sound, flat as a mill pond, was no contest.

Having weighed my options, I chose the Birmingham reservoirs for my Sunday afternoon excursion even though Michael thought the tour might resemble yesterday's ramble too much. In a way it did, but I could hardly get my fill of Welsh vistas on a clear day like today. Birmingham has three reservoirs in Wales for which it pays a ha-penny a gallon, actually less than the water rates in Wales, Marjorie informed me.

Mike parked at one dam so that Marjorie and I could climb a hillside that rose from the parking lot. I had an urge to get out and feel the land beneath my feet. Perhaps I could approach some of the sheep in the field above. We were making pretty good progress through the bracken and slippery moss, leaning heavily into the hillside, when suddenly both of my feet slipped at once and I went face down in the slimy terrain. My slacks and sweater bore witness to the disaster. Obviously I was not as firmly rooted as the trees that grew horizontal to the road.

All too soon the weekend was over and Monday morning I was to say goodbye to Llanidloes once more and especially to Hafod, which is a home where a live wood and coal fire cheers us each afternoon at teatime, tended chiefly by Dorothy; where a pre-dinner gin and tonic is prepared by Marjorie and presented with a "Here's to us," and where Michael periodically interrupts his reading of E. F. Benson to say, "Eve' lyn, have you read..." or, "Have you visited..." and goes off to the bookcase to find Book of British Villages or The Oxford Book of Literary Anecdotes or Powys Homes and Gardens. Hafod is a house of books, books that come off the shelves and pile up around us every evening no matter what the topic of conversation is. Dede Josslyn's Come Early Spring reminded Dorothy of Gillian Clarke's The Sundial. In The Sundial I learn of Dafydd ap Gwilym, a medieval poet, and we are suddenly all discussing medieval ballads, poets, history, churches, and connections.

The conversations revert again and again to Mum, who died only about two years ago at the age of ninety. She liked to play Scrabble with Mike and Marjorie when Dorothy was still teaching off in Cardiff. Mike would study the dictionary all morning looking for unusual words. Mum was chiefly confined to two- and three-letter words like *of* or *sat*. One evening Mike and Marjorie sensed that Mum was suffering mixed emotions. They waited. Finally she defiantly spelled out S H I T, not knowing where to look in her embarrassment.

Hafod is Mrs. Jones across the street, whom I first met in town Saturday morning, and Georgie Thomas, who lives in the house attached to the right of the Worthingtons, and the reverend, who lives in the house attached to their left. And Hafod is "airing closets," designed to keep clothes warm until you put them on. Mike paid four hundred pounds (about $600) two years ago for an airing closet in his flat.

I see and hear magpies and rooks commonly as I walk about Llanidloes... and invariably sheep, sheep up the hillsides, sheep in the bracken, on the rocky outcroppings, in the fields and in the roads. But Monday morning we would say goodbye to all this and return to London.

Michael set departure time for eleven o'clock, giving me time to walk into town, cash some travelers checks and once more stroll around the Old Market Hall. Marjorie was busy in the kitchen packing the lunch we would stop to eat along the way.

Shortly after eleven, with luggage and lunch for four meticulously stowed away, the four of us were off to London. The view was clearer than when we drove down on Friday. Mike and Dor kept quizzing me on what they had told me on the trip to Llanidloes.

"What is Penybont famous for?"

"Horse races by the locals."

"Right!"

We experienced several checkpoints of a motorcycle scramble, noted Northleach, a choice little village built entirely of Cotswold stone, and stopped in Penbridge long enough to spend a penny. At a lay-by just outside of Gloucester, we devoured Marjorie's delicious picnic. And what's a British picnic without piping hot tea from the flask! Then, bless Mike, he left the main road to drive down the High at Burford, another town of Cotswold stone, so that I could see where Barbara and Rachel, some friends from home, had spent their August holiday.

We reached Michael's flat about teatime, and Dorothy had the kettle boiling before Mike had finished carrying the suitcases up four flights to his rooms.

Michael had often through the years spoken of his friend Jo Cox, but I had never met her until that evening. Somehow between teatime and dinner at eight, Mike had managed to put together another of his irresistible meals at which Jo joined us. I was not surprised to find that she shares their same curiosity about things present and their memory of things past and the joy of putting the pieces together. We conversed late into the evening until Marjorie reminded everyone that someone was going to have to get up in the morning and do something about reservations if we expected to get to Belgium on Wednesday.

Getting those reservations took up most of Tuesday. The little travel agency on the corner needed more time than we had and recommended Thomas Cook. So off Marjorie and I went to Thomas Cook Travel Agency at Marble Arch. Because Dorothy's toe was bothering her, she didn't join us but suggested we meet her in Trafalgar Square later for one of St. Martins-in-the-Field's free noontime concerts. She would bring crackers and cheese to nibble if we arrived early. We were to look for her on the wall in front of the National Gallery. Our errand done, Marjorie and I returned to Trafalgar Square and had no trouble finding Dorothy sitting on the wall in the sun. The day was blue and warm. One would have thought as we sat there in front of the National Gallery, stripped down to our shirtsleeves and munching our elevensies that it was midsummer instead of October 4.

The church was respectably filled when we entered for the concert. Nichola Jenkin, a young British soprano, sang selections from Purcell and Mozart with charm and ease and considerable volume. In fact, the whole program was performed with a charm that I had not expected in such a large space.

Dorothy nipped straight home after the concert, while Marjorie and I visited the Manet exhibit in the gallery. It was exceedingly crowded, folks standing three and four deep at most of the pictures. We would have preferred a more leisurely viewing, but we had to return to Marble Arch and Thomas Cook to learn whether our reservations had been made. They had, indeed, and we could pick up our tickets for London to Bruges plus hotel at Time Out, Inc. "next to Victoria."

So off we went again on London Transport to Victoria Station. As it turned out, "next to Victoria" took a little searching and a few inquiries. We found it finally about half a mile from Victoria in a close off Chester Street. It was a darling little office, small, idyllic, done all up in white and blue. A baby's pram in the entry seemed to add just the right touch. Overall, though, it was obviously efficient. We left, confident that all was in order for our departure the next day. By then the rush hour was upon us. We headed back for Mike's without a rewarding tea in St. James Park. Dorothy, however, was home and ready to reward.

The taxi arrived promptly at 8:30 Wednesday morning, allowing time for bottlenecked traffic between Marble Arch and Victoria Station from which we would depart. Despite what we have come to call Worthington anxieties, things proceeded without a misstep. Through Brixton and Peckham Rye, past Catford and Bickley, into Petts Wood and Dutton Green, past Sevenoaks and Tonbridge, the train sped. Perhaps because we would be visiting Ghent in a few days, echoes of "How They Brought the Good News from Ghent to Aix" ran through my head. As Browning tells it:

> I sprang to the stirrup, and Joris, and he;
> I gallop'd, Dirck gallop'd, we gallop'd all three;
> "Good speed!' cried the watch, as the gate-bolts undrew;

"Speed!" echoed the wall to us galloping through;
Behind shut the postern, the lights sank to rest,
And into the midnight we gallop'd abreast.

Well, we weren't galloping. We were click-clacking "all four" along the rails. Nor was it midnight. By the time we reached Tonbridge, it was ten-thirty in the morning. The cows seemed to have eaten their fill. I saw one large herd of Holsteins lying down in a field, as much as to say, "Don't disturb us. We are generating gallons of contented milk." The countryside is not unlike that of the West Country except on a smaller scale. The train flew by sheep, munching in their little portioned squares, and by green fields with newly sprouted winter wheat. Hops fields and oast houses became more common as the train clickity-clacked on, nonstop, through Ashford to Dover.

Ah, Dover! Among the ghosts along its coast I spotted Matthew Arnold. His "Dover Beach" pictures first the tranquil bay:

The sea is calm tonight,
The tide is full, the moon lies fair
Upon the Straits;—on the French coast, the light
Gleams, and is gone; the cliffs of England stand,
Glimmering and vast, out in the tranquil bay.
. . . .
[But] Listen! You hear the grating roar
Of pebbles which the waves draw back, and fling,
At their return, up the high strand,
Begin, and cease, and then begin again,
With tremulous cadence, slow, and bring
The eternal note of sadness in.

Sophocles long ago
Heard it on the Aegean, and it brought
Into his mind the turbid ebb and flow
Of human misery....

However, our little four were too excited—and anticipatory—to feel any misery that day. The jetfoil from Dover to Ostend was comfortable and fast, ninety minutes from pier to pier, but not as dramatic as I had expected. Never having been in a jetfoil before, I am not sure what I thought speeding a few inches over the water would be like. I could have adapted Matthew Arnold:

The sea is calm today,
The tide is full, the sun lies fair. . . .

However, the control kept apologizing for the bad weather. They even suspended distribution of drinks for the first half hour. There we sat, just above the surface of the English Channel, strapped into our seats. In fact, I thought we looked very much like the interior of an airplane. But when we took off, the continuous slapping of the waves against the craft reminded us that we were very close to water. Though we could hear the waves, we scarcely felt them. In a plane the ride would be classified as smooth. We were hardly launched when out came a famous Worthington picnic, complete with tea, of course. The last crumbs were heartily lapped up and the serviettes returned to the basket, than it was time to disembark in Ostend. The train from there to Bruges took fourteen minutes. On leaving the station in Bruges, we were greeted with instant beauty—a park full of bright flowers. Another four minutes by taxi brought us to the Interhotel, Hoefijzerlaan 17-19, 8000 Bruges. We were ready to be discovered.

Having lunched on the jetfoil, we set out immediately, after finding our rooms and depositing our luggage, to orient ourselves—each with a map in hand and a few divergent thoughts in head. Bruges, at that time with a population of 150,000, was a city of canals, churches, spires, flowers, and history. Where to begin? There was, for instance, the Belfry in the Grande Place with a two-hundred-and-sixty-foot tower. My companions showed no immediate interest in climbing the three hundred and thirty-six steps to the top. According to the tourist bureau its carillon with forty-seven bells weighing a total of twenty-seven tons is the most famous in Europe. I will hear its peal from my hotel room. In the course of the afternoon we found the Town Hall, the Government Palace, the fish market, and shops full of lace. By four o'clock we were ready to search out the Old Bruges Tea Room, for which the travel agency had given us complimentary tickets for afternoon tea. The service was impeccable; my hot chocolate, hot and delicious. The chocolate cake was so light it almost floated off the plates. Soft background music included "Greensleeves" sans lyrics.

From tea our amble took us to the Church of our Lady, a spot we will doubtlessly return to throughout our visit, the Cathedral of St. Savior (Saint Salvatorkatedrael) and the Zilverpan. The latter is a group of forty select shops and unique galleries doing a brisk business without ever disturbing or distracting from the medieval architecture around them, all in the shadow of the cathedral tower. In the Zilverpan we noted a tearoom restaurant to which we returned later for supper. Maybe too much later, for we sensed before finishing that they were eager to close. The piped-in music included "Whatever Will Be Will Be; Que Sera Sera," and "Green, Green Grass of Home." My steak was tender, done exactly to my taste with a good béarnaise sauce. No complaints there. Finally we were the last diners remaining and were not encouraged to have tea, coffee or sweets, though Dorothy did have her hot chocolate.

We followed dinner with a walk through a fairy tale of floodlit towers and spires. I went to bed wondering how our train companion from Ostend to Bruges was faring. He was a Swiss lad, spastic and traveling alone, very bright but anxious about connections he had to make at Cologne.

Under Dorothy's leadership we unanimously agreed the next day be devoted to Ghent. A path through a pleasant park led to the station where trains to Ghent run half hourly. Twenty-four minutes later we detrained in a station that from the outside looked more like a palace or a castle than a railroad station. Ghent (population 250,000) being larger than Bruges had more of what most delighted Dorothy, namely, museums and churches, in direct proportion to its larger size. A busy day awaited us. We strolled windowlappingly (a French idiom, Mike says) toward the Centrum, the heart of the old city. There architecture, history, and glories galore were ours to explore. Even though St. Michael's was closed because of vandalism and St. Nicholas' across the street for repairs, St. Bavo's, its belfry tower dominating this city of towers, was open, as was St. John's Cathedral with more towers, contributing to the symphony of the city's towers. The cathedral, though, is best known for its Herbert and Jan Eych's The Mystic Lamb. This large polytych is in two parts, each with a central triptych. In addition, the piece on the left had two extra panels on each side of the triptych—all seven being placed above five additional panels. The four panels to the right rest above four below them, but the central two differ in width from the ones above them. The whole presentation is far too complicated and dramatic to be captured in words. As we sat and studied it, the curator came out about every five or six minutes to close the outer panels, revealing eleven more panels of paintings. The Mystic Lamb, painted in A.D. 1432, is unique in the world of triptychs.

Nestled in a car park on the edge of a canal we found a tiny shop that caters to students. Lunching there gave us an opportunity to enjoy the young folks as well as the food. The canal was lined with former guild houses, a street-long museum in themselves, representing medieval, gothic, and renaissance architecture.

Two mundane observations I made about Ghent are that policepersons are few and public loos for women, nonexistent. Also, the urinals along the side of the cathedral were so exposed that Michael's modesty would not let him use one. Though speaking of the body may be bawdy, I must confess I wondered: how does it feel to ride a bicycle on these cobbled streets of Ghent? The streets were not merely cobbled, they were cobbled artistically—works of art in themselves, and very picturesque with occasional horse-drawn carts clip-clopping by.

After lunch we attended an audio-visual lecture on the history of Ghent as we sat on the edges of a huge model of the city drawn to scale, including the canals and the river Lieve. The spotlighted lecture began with the birth of Charles V in the early sixteenth century and brought the history of Ghent to the present.

We took tram #4 back to the station, thinking all the way that Dorothy would find one more museum we should not resist, but she finally capitulated.

Back in Bruges, we walked to our hotel, detouring by way of the almshouses. School was just letting out. Every student must have a bicycle, and despite the excellent bike paths, many were taking shortcuts along the pedestrian walks.

Dinner that evening was at the Criterium on the walk by what I had dubbed "Red Square." The dining room was spic and span, red and white: the meal, superbly served, leisurely eaten.

The name of what I had been led to believe was the Inter-Hotel turned out to be "De Gouden Boom, prop. Van Herreweghe-Calens." Last evening when we came in the woman at the desk explained that the device in the black containers in our rooms were for flies.

"Flies?" I queried.

"Yes, plug it in where the shaver goes."

Some of the flies were mosquitoes; some were noseeums. Whatever the device was, it did help to alleviate the effects of the invasion which had occurred apparently sometime during the day. Far more important than the invasion, though, were the views from my bedroom window, the juxtaposition of Belfry Tower and Notre Dame. I photographed them both in evening illumination and in morning sunrise. They came out so well that I used one of them for my holiday letter that year.

Belfry Tower and Notre Dame, Bruges

After a continental breakfast of croissant, hard rolls, jams, cheeses, coffee, and orange juice all four of us visited the Church of Our Lady and then bought a comprehensive discount ticket for four museums. The Groeninge, however, was the only one we could get through before the two o'clock closing.

After lunching in the shadow of Belfrey Tower, we decided to each go our separate way. With my comprehensive museum ticket I managed Arentshuis and half of Gruntheuse before, museum-besotted, I gave up and took to the streets in search of whatever they might reveal.

That evening, being Friday and the beginning of the weekend, our hotel restaurant was open to its guests, and we dined on what must have been one of Bruges' best before hurrying off to a concert of trumpet and organ at the cathedral.

Saturday is market day in Bruges, and now I know what I have been calling Red Square is really for. We had two hours between breakfast and leaving for the station. Each went our separate way to pack as much as we could of what we most wanted into the evaporating minutes.

First I walked through the market, taking pictures. Pictures, for instance, of barbecued chickens. One of several such stands had rows upon rows of birds turning on spits. Imagine the aroma! Imagine vehicles, some seventeen meters long, driven into the square and then opened up, unfolded, expanded each into its own private boutique or shop of skinned rabbits hanging above other meats or a shop of nothing but eggs or cheese or sweaters, jewelry, records, shoes, or corsets (for the yet-to-be-liberated woman). The picture I most hoped would come out well was of a man with the oh-so-Belgian face selling nothing but eggs in a little tentlike shelter probably not more than six by twelve feet—nothing but eggs all boxed, row upon row.

Then, what should I do with one hour left in Bruges? I might never be back. The fish market or the Memling Museum that I had skipped yesterday? The streets, so uncrowded and leisurely earlier in the week, were bulging with humanity today. I nudged my way, moving with the stream, wishing for more time to take it all in. Finally the fish market won. It was as lively as the rest of the market. I just stood and watched as the fishmongers wrapped their catch in great strips of white paper and then pages of newspaper—a dozen plaice, ten pounds of turbot, two quarts of prawns. Obviously the Memling would have to wait for another time despite Dorothy's shock that I could forego the masterpieces of Hans Memling housed in the famous St. John's Hospital, which dates from the twelfth century, plus other "precious works of art," the fourteenth-century cloister and the old dispensary.

We had agreed to meet in the lobby, ready to leave, at eleven-fifteen. Nearing the hotel at eleven-fifteen-and-a-half, I heard a voice behind me ask, "What did you do?" It was Dorothy, whom for once Mike could not accuse of being late.

A taxi whisked us to the station, where a train for Ostend was waiting. We had allowed an hour for a snack in Ostend (and to ease Mike's anxieties about missing the jetfoil). With an hour and a half before we were scheduled to leave, we were surprised to be asked whether we would like to board the jetfoil at the pier on the verge of departing. It had been delayed by technical problems but was now ready for departure. Without missing a footstep and only waving our passports, we were hurried aboard. By then we were two hours ahead of schedule and assured of good light for viewing the white cliffs of Dover and Dover Castle upon our arrival in England.

> There'll be blue birds over
> The white cliffs of Dover
> Tomorrow;
> Just you wait and see.
>
> There'll be love and laughter
> And peace ever after
> Tomorrow:
> Just you wait and believe.

We taxied to Mike's flat, pronounced the continental venture a great success, settled into Mike's cheese soufflé and our trip-quiz game with a sense of accomplishment and contentment. I would be leaving for home soon, confident that my sentimental journey with the Worthingtons had truly "set my heart at ease."

Hardy's Own Tess

I WAS JUST PREPARING a pickled herring sandwich for lunch when the phone rang. When I answered, a voice said, "Eve-lynn? Is that you?"

"Di!" I exclaimed, recognizing her accent and the customary British two-syllable pronunciation of my name. "What's the occasion?"

After some preliminary chatter, Diana said, "I'm calling because BBC is going to interview Mum for a TV broadcast about Hardy, and she wants you to come go with us to Southampton for the taping. What do you say?"

"At the moment I am too surprised to say anything," I replied. "When's this going to happen?"

"Next month. How about it? Do say yes. We'd both be ever so pleased to have you."

"Right on the spot I can't think of any reason why not. But you know me. My phlegmatic nature can't respond immediately. It's my nature to deliberate. But I can tell you the little wheels are beginning to whirr." We chatted for a while and finally closed the conversation with my promise to think what all was involved and to get back to her soon.

"Very soon, mind you!"

I was retired from teaching. My calendar was pretty fluid. I hadn't been to Great Britain for four or five years. What's to hinder? I thought. Actually, I suspect that I really knew from the moment Di asked what my answer would be.

Every crossword puzzle buff is acquainted with the definition "Hardy's heroine (four letters)." The answer, Tess, in real life is Gertrude Bugler, Diana's mum. My friendship with Gertrude, Trudy to her friends, went back many years. When I first met her, she had been visiting relatives in Canada and had been persuaded to stop in Toronto on her return to New York, from where she would be sailing home. She had a prearranged meeting at the university with Michael Millgate, a Hardy scholar. He was collecting letters of Thomas Hardy with the intent of publishing them and had questions to discuss with Gertrude concerning the chronology of some events. She had also agreed to meet Professor Carl Weber at Colby College in Waterville, Maine, who was writing a biography of Hardy. Then she would stop in Fairfield, where I was teaching, to visit a colleague of mine who had discovered her the previous summer during a ramble through Hardy's Wessex. In other words this was a woman sought out by folks interested in knowing someone who had known Thomas Hardy. This was the woman who was billed as "Hardy's Own Tess" when in 1929 she played the lead in Tess of the D'Ubervilles at the Duke of York Theatre in London.

First of all, by the 1960s Mrs. Bugler was one of a very few still living who had known Hardy. Furthermore she had played the lead in a number of his novels that had been dramatized and presented to the public by the Hardy Players, members of the Dorchester Debating and Dramatic Society.

Trudy's dramatic flare first came to Hardy's attention in 1913. Mr. Tilley, of the Hardy Players, had seen Trudy play Adam in a high school production of Shakespeare's As You Like It and was so impressed he recommended she be invited to play Marty South in the dramatization of Hardy's The Woodlanders. She was invited and accepted, though she had never read The Woodlanders. Thus fate brought her and Thomas Hardy together. She was then sixteen; he, seventy-three. She recalls his attending a rehearsal one evening and though she does not know where she found the courage to approach the famous novelist, she asked his advice on just how she should deliver Marty South's lament at the end of the play. He merely replied, "Oh, you will know how when the moment comes. Just say it as you feel it." And she did. The applause was heart-warming.

Seven years later when the Hardy Players chose The Return of the Native for their annual presentation, Gertrude was a natural for the part of Eustacia. Although Hardy had had no particular woman in mind when he wrote the novel, he said she was exactly what he had pictured, "tall and dark." He was also taken with her "beautifully modulated voice." On one occasion during the rehearsals for The Return of the Native, she was invited with the rest of the cast for tea at Max Gate, Hardy's home in Dorchester. That was the first of several visits.

In the next eight years (until his death in 1928) Gertrude had several memorable opportunities to be in his company and to talk with him. Shortly before his death at the age of eighty-eight she was visiting in his home. When she left that evening, he walked with her down the curving driveway to her car. On the way he said, "If anyone should ever ask whether you knew Thomas Hardy, say, 'Yes, he was my friend.' " That was the last time she saw him. It is also one of her fondest recollections.

This was the Gertrude Bugler who was inviting me twenty-plus years after our first meeting to go with her for her interview with BBC. Of course, I accepted. The occasion for the broadcast was the fifty-fifth anniversary of Hardy's death.

Trudy as Eustacia in Return of the Native

Three weeks after our telephone conversation I was on a Pan Am flight headed for London, where I spent a couple of days with my Welsh friend Mike before moving on to Beaminster in Dorset, and Trudy. Mike's sister Dorothy came up from Wales for my brief visit, for we three never miss an opportunity to share a cuppa and some good conversation.

"Now with this whole day and a half you are giving us," Dorothy said impishly at breakfast, "what do you want to do with it?" We had sat up and talked for hours after I arrived the night before. With my biological watch still on USA time, I was feeling more alert than they were when Mike's chimes struck 3 A.M.

"Well, for starters," I asked, "what's on at the National Gallery?"

"That's an idea," Dorothy said. "The Manet exhibit has been getting extravagant reviews."

"I have tickets for Toussaint tonight," Mike reminded us.

"If there's time after the National Gallery, we could amble over to Festival Hall. Something's always going on there," added Dorothy.

After visiting the National Gallery we wandered through Trafalgar Square. How different I felt from my visit on New Year's Eve, 1954, when I stood watching the shenanigans in the pools and refusing to admit I was homesick. That was the visit when I bought my Morris Minor. Six years later I bought the Hillman Minx in London and traveled all over Great Britain with Winnie and Phyllis, Marion and my cousin Mary—not all at the same time. My next trip was Clare's first visit to Europe, a trip that after Amsterdam, Paris, and London climaxed in Beaminster for a two-day visit with Trudy. And in 1979 after our art tour through Italy, Clare and I had come to England again, where we witnessed Margaret Thatcher's inaugural parade when she became prime minister and Clare talked with the bobby whose picture she took and later painted. After London, of course, we went to Dorset to visit Trudy Bugler, as I would be doing tomorrow. So many memories! And through all these visits my friendship with Trudy had grown.

The pigeons and the traffic in Trafalgar Square that day as I walked with Dorothy and Mike seemed thicker than ever—- Indians, Japanese, Jamaicans; blacks, yellows, and whites; old and young; healthy and halt; lovers and lonelies. And the pigeons, as always, fluttered and perched everywhere, including on my head. That's why I was wearing a cap.

Before I knew it, it was Saturday morning. Mike served a proper British breakfast complete with tomatoes, bacon, eggs, and lots of toast and orange marmalade. "What you'd call brunch in the States, being served at this hour," Dorothy observed. Then Mike, bless him, was ready to drive me to Waterloo Station to catch the train for Crewherne where Diana would meet me.

I remember well the ride that morning. Once beyond London and the suburbs, fields—both harvested and being harvested—flashed past us (when high hedges permitted.) A herd of cows on a country road bespoke the rustic scenes I was anticipating in Dorset. I remember we passed a semidetached, stuccoed house painted one half white and the other half purple. Live and let live, I thought to myself. There followed an industrial park, and then some fields of Holsteins and Herefords. The latter were a promise of the open farmland I would find in Dorset. My traveling companion turned out to be interesting—and interested. We touched upon a number of subjects during the two-and-a-half hour trip. She told me she was "thrilled...a little bit" that she was to be included in An Anthology of Nursing.

Diana gave me her usual warm welcome when I stepped from the train.

"Where's your luggage?" she asked.

"Here," I indicated, pointing to my knapsack.

"Righto! Then let's be on our way," and we were soon on the road to Beaminster some five miles away.

"Mum didn't come along. She's napping. She's had an unexpected visitor, Betsy Ross of Canada, the past two days. They do pop up without much notice. They'll only stay an hour, they say, and then stay two or three. The two gentlemen from Japan were here again last month. Funny little chaps—those Japs. But Mum thrives on all the activity."

"I've lost track of her age. Eighty-four was it last March?"

"Eighty-six!"

"You'd never guess it. 'S strange the keen interest the Japanese have in Hardy. I wonder how Jude the Obscure looks in Japanese."

"Or sounds. But Mum wants you to come for tea. She'll be up and rarin' to talk with you by then. She's more excited about your visit than she is the taping tomorrow."

Trudy had grown up in Hardy's hometown of Dorchester, but moved to Beaminster, one of my very favorite British villages, when she married in 1921. The guidebook describes it as "set among steep farmland hills." The stone houses are mostly eighteenth century, built of the golden (now gone a little gray) Ham Hill stone of the region. A little stream runs along the side of Main Street and past Riverside Cottage, where Trudy first lived when she came to Beaminster as a bride. Not large, the river trickles rather than runs through the village, trickles and sparkles.

In the heart of town is a market cross. I was getting goose bumps as Diana approached it, anticipating her turning at the cross onto Church Street. We passed Number 3, Woodbury House, Trudy's home, and continued down the street so narrow two cars could scarcely meet. At the bottom Di turned left, climbing a short distance to her home, Tower Hill, next to the great gray-stoned church and churchyard.

"We'll settle you in first, though you haven't much to settle, and then do some tongue wagging of our own before we go to tea. Mum will be looking for us. I'll give her a ring in a little to tell her you are here and to put the kettle on."

However, Trudy rang first. "Come along," she said. "Tea will be ready by the time you get here."

We walked the short distance along the narrow cobbled lane to the stone steps of Woodbury House, steps that come to the street's edge. Before we could say "Canonacoram," we were nattering away over tea and scones as though I dropped in every afternoon.

Trudy was as excited as ever about Hardy. She had a copy of the new biography by Michael Millgate, her Toronto connection, inscribed to her and signed by Michael himself. "Much better than Robert Gittings," she thought. "Better balanced. He sticks to facts, doesn't indulge in speculation." She was excited, too, about Gordon Beningfield's new book, his paintings of the Hardy countryside. Trudy had recently met Beningfield at an exhibition in the Dorset Museum. He was planning an expanded edition of his current book with quotations from Hardy's poems and novels to accompany the paintings. The friendship between the two was almost instantaneous. She had much to tell me about him. Trudy and I talked about visitors who continue to beat a path to her door to discuss the Hardy she knew. They come not only from Great Britain but also Canada, Iceland, Japan, America, and beyond.

Gertrude Bugler and daughter Di

Once tea was finished, Di washed up and left for home, reminding us that supper would be served at half-seven at Tower Hill and not to be late. She reminded us also of the time some years before when Trudy was to visit J. O. Bailey at the University of North Carolina. She had been engaged to spend a few days on campus, meet with some of his students, and talk about Hardy. Calm as Trudy appears on the outside this was an awesome challenge, not the meeting of strangers (she already knew Professor Bailey) but the intricacies of international travel. I offered to meet her flight at La Guardia and drive her to the Port Authority in the city, where she would get a bus to North Carolina. First of all her plane was late, a situation that was upsetting in itself, and if I remember right it was raining. "I'm too old for this sort of thing," Trudy said as we made our way to my car. "Folks don't realize I'm only a country maid. I should never have left Beaminister." She wiped away a tear.

"Everything is going to be all right," I assured her, pulling out into traffic. Progress was slow, as it usually is, getting away from the airport and across the city. Once the car was parked, we had about forty minutes before the bus left. Trudy clutched her ticket as we sat on a bench and waited. Di never lets us forget that we became so engrossed in conversation that her mum missed the bus. Anyway, another bus was leaving for the South in two hours, and I waited with her until it departed.

I met her in New York on her return and whisked her off for a visit with me in Fairfield, but that's another story. Tonight was supper with Diana. And then early to bed. Tomorrow would be a big day for all of us.

When Diana went to fetch Trudy Sunday morning, she exclaimed, "I thought we had it fixed you'd wear your blue dress!"

To which Mum replied indignantly, "I'm not going to wear that dress in the morning!" So Di packed the blue dress, which Mum later would be persuaded to change into. The pealing of St. Peter's bells greeted us as we approached Dorchester. At the intersection the Lord Mayor's procession, some fifteen or more robed dignitaries, was rounding the corner to enter the church, a very colorful sight.

Our journey continued through Tolpuddle and Puddletown. A half-mile farther east Trudy pointed out Athelhampton Hall. "It's one of the famous manor houses of Great Britain," she informed me. "We might as well pack in a little history as we ride along, don't you think?"

"You can give the lecture, Mum," Di said, "but we have no time for tours."

"Nor do I want any. Not today."

Near Wimborne we passed World's End Inn, which I was told was where Eisenhower with others plotted Dunkirk. Some heather was showing a little mauve as we drove through New Forest, but the wild ponies were scarce and fenced in, not running loose as I saw and photographed them when I first came to England. "They became too much of a hazard," Di explained. "They would stand in the road and motorists stopped to feed them. They were such beggars. Then, too, motorists didn't seem to drive so fast in those days. Accidents increased; there was nothing for it but to separate ponies and motorists."

Eventually we reached Southampton and the old Southwestern House, once an elegant hotel where the wealthy stayed before departing Southampton on the old Queens. Today BBC televises The Cellar Show from its cellar. Where else? Among the many attendants to gather around Trudy when she entered was Philip Peale. His great uncle, I learned sometime during the afternoon, captained the Queen Mary. The other tidbit I picked up was that he was once engaged to a young woman from Connecticut, but when she couldn't get a work permit for Great Britain, the engagement was dissolved. Makes you wonder, doesn't it?

The Cellar Show was filmed before a live audience of about a hundred. Before Trudy's interview (and after she had changed into the blue afternoon dress) we sat upstairs and watched on a monitor the filming of the Yetties, who will share the thirty-minute show. Three young men from Yetminster, a tiny village in Dorset, they have sung Hardy folk songs all over the world—in Greece, Norway, Nepal, the Sudan, Tailand, Hong Kong, Singapore, and more.

Finally, long after the appointment hour of noon, John Sessions, actor and comedian, was ready to interview Trudy. After all the waiting and anticipating, she was tired and in a bit of a tizzy. Sympathetically, Sessions started with a few throwaway questions and in no time Trudy settled down, lost in her memories of Thomas Hardy. She spoke calmly and clearly in the dramatic, melodious voice for which she was famous. The questions were so worded that Trudy had a chance to portray Hardy as she wished the world to know him, for she never missed an opportunity to say he was not the pessimist so many people thought him. The last question turned the discussion to Trudy herself.

"Why do you think the theater billed you as 'Hardy's Own Tess' when Tess of the D'Ubervilles played for six months in London? In what sense were you his Tess?"

After thinking a moment she said, "Well, when Mr. Hardy wrote the novel—years before it was dramatized—-he modeled Tess on a dairymaid he remembered having seen on a Dorset farm when he was young. Then I have been told, though he never mentioned it to me, that when he saw me performing The Woodlanders when I was in high school, he remarked to someone, 'That's my Tess,' meaning, of course, the Tess, 'the tall dark woman' he had modeled Tess on in his novel. Or," she deliberated, "maybe the company was apologizing for bringing an amateur actor to the London stage. I had had no training as an actress, no elocution lessons." Laughing, she added, "At least I had the dialect right."

Experts, scholars, and other interested folk have pretty much come to an agreement in recent years that the "tall dark woman" Hardy remembered was actually Gertrude Bugler's mother, Augusta Way. Mrs. Way was a dairy maid and close neighbor of the Hardy's at Bockhampton. In fact Hardy's brother Harry and Augusta's brother Fred were close friends. Those who knew both Trudy and her mother said that the two were very alike in almost every way.

The live audience loved Trudy and crowded around when the taping was over. As always she was generous in listening to and she was generous in answering their questions.

We returned home via the old Roman Road out of Dorchester. One-car wide between hedges two and three times higher than the car, the road goes straight as an arrow and passes "on the top" a prehistoric barrow, at last dipping down, down, down to "nights in the bottom." Until recently Diana thought it was "knights (with a k) in the bottom" but has learned it is a place where drovers herded their cattle overnight while they stayed in a pub nearby. Should one meet another car on the Roman Road and not be near one of the occasional half a half dollar turnouts, one or the other must back to a turnout. The British are polite about offering to reverse.

I woke the next morning thinking about a Hardy story the Yetties had told. It is called "Absent-minded in the Village Choir." I have since then acquired a copy, or version, of it in a booklet entitled "A 'Mellstock Quire' Boy's Recollection of Thomas Hardy." The incident happened when the bored quire took to nipping during a Sunday sermon, fell asleep, missed their cue and came to thinking they were playing for the Saturday night folk dance. The squire was not amused. Henceforth a barrel organ of psalms replaced the boys' choir.

At breakfast Trudy confessed she had "simmered through last night" regretting that in her interview she had neglected to say that Hardy was a realist, a point she always stressed whenever anyone called him a pessimist.

"But you did say it," I told her.

"Oh? Then that's all right." Matter settled. Anxiety put to rest.

• • •

When I confirmed that yes I would come for the televising in Southampton, Diana had said, "And you will stay a week. . .or more?"

"Hardly that long," I replied. "You know what folks say about a fish or a guest after three days."

"That doesn't apply when you come across the ocean to visit, and you know it. And it certainly does not apply when you come to see us. And you know that, too."

"Enough ands," I said, laughing. "I'll compromise—not that I wouldn't like to stay throughout the autumn. I'll stay until midweek." Now after the trip to Southampton, I was sticking to my resolve. Trudy was tired, as I knew she would be. Therefore, I announced after breakfast that I was going off by myself for the day. The sun shone brightly in a heavenly blue sky. Meals on wheels would bring Trudy her lunch and Diana was waiting for two cats to be picked up from her cattery. I said what I would really like to do was browse in a few shops (It was early closing day), cash a check, buy some postcards, write in my diary, buy a savory, and walk, walk, walk out beyond the village. I'd have my own private picnic out there somewhere with the cows. That was fine with Di, but Trudy was appalled. I explained that I always promised myself one solitary excursion wherever I visited. Promising Trudy that I would be back for tea in her garden and reminding her that I was treating her and Di to dinner at the Acorn in Evershot that evening, I went on my way—camera, diary, and pens in my belly pack. I would buy my picnic in the village.

It was noon before I knew it, past noon and time for my picnic. But just where was I going to have it? I walked on a little farther. Then, bless those Brits: they know a walker needs a breather now and then, if not to rest, at least to pause and admire the view. Within another half mile I came upon a bench in a bend of the road. I hadn't realized how high I had climbed until I looked back at the village still visible there in the bottom, surrounded by green fields. From where I stood, I could have blotted it all out—the village and total population of eight hundred—with a shilling held at arm's length. Taking possession of the bench, I set about writing postcards, bringing my diary up to date, and munching my cheddar cheese, meat pie and Bell's scotch lunch. In the next hour, two cars went by, and four crows. No walkers. The woman in the first car smiled and I waved. After lunch I took some pictures and sat a little longer, watching the mists grow in the valley. The top of my scotch bottle said, "Afore you go."

I thought of Trudy and wondered whether "the boys" had come as promised to wash her front windows. I thought, too, of Diana and wondered whether the cats had been collected. Di adores cats and is a natural mother to them. When her husband Philip walked out on her and their two children, Di was desolate until her son Michael suggested a cattery. She took to the idea like a cat to catnip. She can accommodate sixteen cats, each with private quarters, its own name on the door, plush bright orange beds, a plastic dust bin for a retreat, cat walks, scratch boards, and toys—its own if it wants to bring them. Currently she has three cats in residence plus Pickles, who was just twitching and clawing to escape when Diana arrived with her straight from the vet's for a few days of rehab after being spayed. The cattery is so popular that owners make reservations months ahead when they plan their vacations, and at least a year ahead for holidays.

The sun was headed for the yardarm when I decided to relinquish the roadside bench to whatever hiker might follow me. I would have to freshen up before going to Trudy's for tea, and later, dinner. Trudy was all for going to the Acorn when Di suggested it last night, but by breakfast this morning she had changed her mind.

"I'm too old, too deaf, too slow," she grumbled at breakfast. That was one of my clues that she didn't need me around today to entertain. Had I been there, we would have talked ourselves out the door and over the hill and collapsed long before teatime.

I replied, "I want you to go, no matter how miserable you will be!" How she laughed.

She said, "Some people think I am miserable, but I can still laugh."

At tea I learned dinner would be at Bridge House in the Square instead of the Acorn because the mists had not dissipated, and the seven miles from Evershot after dinner could be tedious (Trudy's word) returning in the dark. We could walk to the Bridge House almost across from Trudy's home. Di was chortling when I arrived. "Mum just phoned not to ask what she should wear to dinner but to get approval of what she had already decided to wear. One has to be careful at her age not to let others make decisions for you."

"I don't think there's any danger anyone will make Trudy's," I said. "As keen as she is, she will not be shy about asserting herself. I think she is perfectly wonderful, but I don't need to tell you that." And off we went for dinner at the Bridge House.

When Diana returned from the cattery Tuesday morning, she had three of the biggest apples I think I've ever seen. She had plucked them from her own tree in the garden. Their aroma wafted across the table where I sat writing in my diary. I wish I had a way of recording British odors—perhaps no different from those at home but memorable in an unfamiliar setting. Mustiness is a common and to me not unpleasant smell. I associate it especially with old churches and some inns I have been in. But my favorite inn smell on a cold, wet day is that of wood burning in the open fireplace. Yesterday the tar in Long Street was wonderfully pungent, and memorable perhaps because so much renovation and construction work here is done manually. The wheelbarrow has a prominent place. The bakeries, too, have a distinctive aroma, the smell of their many savories—meat pies, mutton pies, sausage pies, their scones, biscuits, tarts. Even the bread smells different.

By Tuesday we had all recovered enough from our trip to Southampton to plan a picnic. Trudy had a place and route in mind that she wanted to share with me. While Di set about organizing the picnic (she had refused my help), I was scanning the morning paper when I came upon this item, which amused me. John Betjeman, Great Britain's poet laureate, had suffered a severe heart attack last week. This morning the press was happy to report he was much improved "thanks to floods of letters from well wishers and the cheerful companionship of his teddy bear, Sebastian."

About noon we set off, Di driving, Trudy guiding. Trudy hoped the sun, which had been teasing all morning, would emerge to reveal the grand views for which the county is so famous. She chose the route, traveling the high-hedged byways. Di even discovered a village or two she had never seen before. We went through Stoke Abbott, another charming town made of the local, yellow Ham Hill stone. In the distance the dim outline of Hackthorn Hill, an 800-foot rise out of Toller Down, showed through the mist. The tallest hill in the county is just a few feet short of one thousand, the height at which a hill qualifies to be called a mountain.

We drove through Shove Cross and Pilsdon, Charmouth, Wooton Fitzpaine and Whitchurch Canonacoram—all in the Marshwood Vale. Love those names! Wild blackberries along the roadside tempted us out of the car. A robin redbreast on a coil of barbed wire complained, "I was saving those berries for friends who are coming to tea a little later." A herd of Herefords had gathered beside the Char.

Lambert Castle, our destination, is a fortification that dates back to 500 B.C. During the Napoleonic Wars beacons transmitted messages from height to height. From Lambert Castle they reached London in ten minutes. Trudy and I spread the blanket while Diana brought the sandwiches, tomatoes, apples, cheese, and biscuits for our picnic. We might have with a little imagination passed for the three witches of Macbeth. I was amazed at Trudy's agility in taking her place on the blanket. Gorse in full bloom surrounded our picnic area. Michael says gorse is always in bloom. He told me there's a saying, "When the gorse is out of bloom, kissing's out of fashion." I wished I were a painter. The camera cannot do justice to the scene, the ruins of the castle, the vivid yellow of the gorse, and the beech grove in the background. What I did take pictures of were huge spider webs bending under the weight of dewdrops from the mist.

The sun beat down upon us as we sat munching cucumber sandwiches, tomatoes, and our cheese and biscuits. The autumn day was mellow. Trudy's thoughts went back to our first meeting. "Winnie came to fetch me in Lewiston, Maine," she mused. "I was spending a few days with my nephew Derek after visiting relatives in Canada and then Carl Weber at Colby. I didn't meet you until I reached Fairfield. You were both teaching English in the same school as I remember."

"And Winnie and I persuaded you to record some of Hardy's poems for us to share with students when we taught Return of the Native or The Mayor of Casterbridge."

"So they made you work for your board and room," Diana commented.

"Oh, that was no chore."

I explained how we tried to bring Egdon Heath to life for students when they read Return of the Native, how I had taken pictures of the heath on my first visit to England, of the single road running through it like a part in a head of dark hair, to quote Hardy, and the desolation that so oppressed Eustacia Vye. "Do you remember, of course you do, the poem in which Hardy said that scene would never change?"

> Only a man harrowing clods
> In a slow silent walk,
> With an old horse that stumbles and nods
> Half asleep as they stalk.
>
> Only thin smoke without flame
> From the heaps of couch grass;
> Yet this will go onward the same
> Though Dynasties pass.
>
> Yonder a maid and her wight
> Come whispering by;
> War's annals will fade into night
> Ere their story dies,

Trudy recited it without a blink.

We all sat meditatively after the recitation, thinking our own thoughts. Then Trudy said, "Ironically, what Hardy thought would 'go onward the same/ Though Dynasties pass,' turned out quite differently. He did not foresee the huge tractors and vast fields of today. And rarely are the beautiful shire horses used today. They are an endangered species. Just a few of the real old country farmers keep a horse more out of sentiment than anything else.

"Yes," she continued, "after that first visit I knew we would become friends. You and Winnie delivered me after two weeks to my ship in New York, waiting at bay in the Hudson River. I thought, I shall return someday to Connecticut, as we stood there together on the deck until the call came, 'All ashore who are going ashore.' "

"But you never came by ship again."

"No, always by plane, and you always met me at the airport."

"Another time you came and I arranged for you to meet the volunteer librarians in our elementary schools. You talked with them about Hardy and recited some of his poems."

"Oh, I do remember that. I had come from a session with J.O. Bailey in North Carolina. You and Clare met me at the Port Authority in New York. My, that seems donkey years ago. The dogwood was in bloom in Fairfield. I'll never forget that. Our meeting with the librarians was at a school on Greenfield Hill. I met Margaret Farquhar, head librarian, and on another day had lunch with her and friends at her home amidst the dogwood. I still have a photo someone took of me that day under a dogwood tree."

Trudy at Margaret's home

"What I remember of that visit is that you had a new dress, approved by Diana, but about which you had some doubts because it barely covered your knees when you sat down."

"I remember that. Wasn't I an old fussbudget about it. That was the visit when I first met Clare, and two or three years later you and Clare came to me at Woodbury House and stayed a night or two. She liked my cat Itsy, even if he did insist on sleeping on her bed."

"You would have driven us to Beeny Cliff had it not been so far away." Beeny Cliff is a headland in Cornwall, looking out across the often stormy Atlantic. It is of special interest to Hardy scholars because of the poem he wrote about going there early in his acquaintance with Emma Gifford. He had gone to Cornwall as an architect in connection with the restoration of a church and while there fell in love with Emma, the rector's sister-in-law. Eventually they married. "Instead of Beeny Cliff you drove Clare and me to Portland Bill, overlooking the English Channel, just a pleasant afternoon drive from Beaminister. How the wind did blow as we tried to eat our picnic and take pictures."

Trudy and I reminisced the afternoon away there among the gorse until Diana suggested we gather up the picnic and think about taking to the road again.

The route from Lambert Castle home passed through the village of Hawkschurch with its white, pink, and yellow stucco houses along one side of the main street and beautiful plantings around the church on the other. I tried to imagine living in such a tidy, pretty spot. We came, too, through Thorncombe, Chard, and Windwhistle. Thomas Hardy, Trudy told me, once stopped for a cup of tea at a pub in Windwhistle and was told that the nearest tea water was a half-mile distance. Would he settle for something a little stronger?

"And did he?" I asked when she paused.

"It is presumed he did."

Wednesday began with my usual cuppa in bed followed later by orange juice and toast with Diana.

"Are you sure you won't stay another day or two?" Di asked, pushing the marmalade jar my way.

"Can't do," I replied resolutely. "I told Mike I would be back in London for a few days, and I want to visit Helen Layton with whom I lived when I was in Oxford forty years ago." Diana was driving me to Crewkerne to catch the 10:33 to London. Trudy had risen early to go with us. I popped my last postcards into the pillar box on the High while Di checked out the cattery. Then we picked up Trudy and were off on the now familiar road to the station.

"I'm going to miss your tiddeley lanes as you call them," I remarked as we rounded a blind corner, "and the intriguing names of your villages," I added. "What was that one not far from Yetminster? Ryme something?"

"Ryme Intrinsica," Trudy supplied. "There used to be a jingle about some of those names. It went something like this, if I can remember,

Ryme Intrinsica, Fontmell Magna,
Sturminster Newton and Melbury Bubb
Whist upon whist upon whist upon whist
Drive, in Institute, Legion and Social Club.

Or something like that," she said, laughing.

In leaving, I remarked that when I retire—ultimately retire—I am going to settle in Beaminister. Trudy replied that I could have her upstairs, that she rarely uses it any more. And we left it at that. She was eighty-six last March 8 and obviously still very bright and alert. She is off next month for California to visit her great grandchildren for six weeks. As I hugged her and climbed aboard the London train, I could not help wondering, though, when we would meet again.

Actually it was only two years later that I had an occasion to spend an afternoon with her. Two New England friends of mine had rented a home for the summer in Frome near Bath and asked whether I would come for a week or two to drive for them. And I did. They were both teachers of English. My tales of Hardy's Tess piqued their curiosity to the point that they suggested we make a literary pilgrimage to visit her. I phoned Diana only to learn that she was in the midst of redecorating. "We are in an awful mess, Eve," she told me, "but of course we want to see you. Not today, or tomorrow, though. How about next Tuesday?

"Are you sure? We don't want to be a nuisance."

"No, Tuesday will be fine. I will have finished the downstairs by then. Do come. Mum will be ever so pleased, as, of course, I will be too."

"And no fussing. We will stay only an hour. I know that is what all the Hardy fans say, but I mean it. We will come shortly after lunch, so don't even think of food."

Since I had last seen Trudy, she had sold Woodbury House and moved in with Diana at Tower Hill. She had an upstairs bedroom with plenty of space for her Hardy memorabilia.

On the afternoon of our visit, introductions and the how-are-yous were scarcely completed before, to no one's surprise, Thomas Hardy's name came up.

"What was it like to know an honest-to-goodness, successful novelist face-to-face?" Barbara asked.

"Well, you must understand I was an unread teenager when I first met him and he was an elderly gentleman who had already written his novels, established his reputation throughout the kingdom. The Hardy Players presented his plays both in Dorchester and in Weymouth. All sorts of important folks came from as far away as London. One evening before a performance Mrs. Hardy sought me out to meet a Colonel Somebody. I didn't get the name, perhaps because I was puzzling over why she said colonel when he was obviously wearing the uniform of a private. Later a member of the cast said to me, 'Did you know you were talking to Lawrence of Arabia?' That's what it was like to know Thomas Hardy. He often introduced me to friends who came for the plays, but the names E.M. Forester, J.M. Barrie (before he was Sir), or Siegfried Sassoon meant nothing to me. I was very much sitting on the sidelines, often not even knowing what I was watching. But he was a dear man and always very considerate of me.

"It was not unusual for him to turn up at a rehearsal. I remember in one of the plays he led us through the figures of an old country dance. Another time he played his violin to help us with a dance. Mr. Hardy remembered the dancers going round the village when he was a boy, and how, when they had finished they would consume quantities of cider. The tunes and dances still ran in his head even as an old man.

"You see I was only thirty-one when he died, and now I'm nearly ninety. For nearly two-thirds of my life I have enjoyed telling folks about the man who said, 'If anyone asks whether you knew Thomas Hardy, say yes, he was my friend.' They come from all over. Snoebjorn Jonsson was here from Iceland just a few weeks ago. He comes rather frequently, an old man, a few months older than myself. I might say, too, if you will forgive an old woman her immodesty, he brought a poem he had written, titled 'Gertrude Bugler.' If you will excuse me a moment, I'd like to share it with you." Off she went, sprightly as could be, up the stairs to her Hardy mementos.

She returned shortly and handed us Jonsson's poem written in Icelandic and translated into English. I quote here the last two of the five stanzas:

> Rich in the gold of the heart as Tess; graceful and
> majestic as Eustacia. Shall not this long be
> remembered? Long will they live. Your name has
> been enshrined in prose and in verse.
>
> Yes, England and Iceland will preserve your name,
> Time ultimately accords to everyone his and her due.
> You were Thomas Hardy's greatest interpreter. Now,
> Gertrude, accept here the token of my gratitude.

"Was Hardy really as pessimistic as his writings suggest?" Barbara asked.

"Good heavens, no," Trudy replied, always happy to point out that he was a realist, fascinated with the irony of circumstances. "He was a happy person, a little shy and like many writers, often withdrawn. He always seemed smiling and happy, kindly, and encouraging. I have a letter upstairs that will show you the kind of man he was. If you will excuse again, I will fetch it." And off she went again up the stairs. She returned with a typewritten copy of what has come to be known among Hardy scholars as The 1920 Christmas letter. She proceeded to read it in part:

Max Gate,
Dec. 26th, 1920

Dear Mr. Cockerell, (a literary friend of T.H.)

We, contrary to our usual custom, have spent a most exciting Christmas. Yesterday the Mummers (under our beloved Mr. Tilley) came and performed in the drawing room, to the intense joy of T. H., his brother and sister (whom I had here) and the rest of the household. And friends who accompanied them fiddled to us and sang carols outside—the real old Bockhampton carols. Then they came in, had refreshments in the dining room and we had a very delightful time with them, Miss Bugler [our Trudy and Hardy's Tess] looking prettier than ever in her mumming dress...

"Oh, dash!" she said, "I meant to stop short of that, but she did write it, didn't she? I wanted to get to the end where Mrs. Hardy continues:

T. is very well. At the party (of the mummers etc.) last night he was so gay –and one of them said to me he had never seen him so young and happy and excited. He is now this afternoon writing a poem with great spirit: always a sign of well-being with him.
Yours very sincerely,
(signed) Florence Hardy

The first dramatization of Return of the Native had taken place just a month before the party Mrs. Hardy refers to here. The players from that production came to Hardy's home at Max Gate on Christmas to please Mr. Hardy by reviving the medieval custom.

"That mummers play has always seemed such a neat device to get Eustacia Vye and Clym Yeobright together," Rachel observed.

"Yes, and it is an example of Hardy's keen interest in the Middle Ages. Other examples of that interest turn up throughout his novels. He called mumming a fossilized survival from medieval times into his own childhood, and then his fiction."

"And right into our conversation here this afternoon," Barbara pointed out. "My students loved the mummers. They played the parts, belting out:

Here come I, a Turkish Knight,
Who learnt in Turkish land to fight;

I'll fight this man with courage bold.
If his blood's hot I'll make it cold!"

"Are mummers plays still performed as they apparently were in Hardy's day?" Rachel asked.

"No," Trudy said, "and they were already a thing of the past in Hardy's day. In fact, when Eve asked donkey years ago whether I could get any pictures of a mummers play, I had a hard time finding any performers."

"But you did, and I have a fine set of slides that have been shown to many students in the States."

At this point Diana came into the room to ask whether anyone would like a tour of her cattery. Barb would, but Rachel, no friend to cats, said she'd rather talk with Trudy about Hardy. The ensuing conversation ranged from his poetry to the people who used to come to Dorchester to visit Hardy or attend the dramatization of his novels. "Many people came from London—frequently, to see the plays," Trudy told Rachel, "and at least twice that I heard of the Prince of Wales was a guest at Max Gate. There are pictures somewhere." At Rachel's request, Trudy read a few poems from the Hardy collection that sat beside her chair.

By the time Barbara returned from the cattery, two hours had flown since our arrival. We were as bad as all those other fans. They promise not to stay but always do. Trudy protested she was not tired and Di insisted we stay for a cup of tea. We stayed.

Diana is an irresistible hostess, and I knew when she brought the teacake in that she had baked it especially for us. Such wonderful friends!

Trudy was a prodigious letter writer. For the next five or six years our letters crossed the Atlantic fairly regularly. Hers brought news of visitors to Tower Hill. Gordon Beningfield, her Wessex artist friend, was one faithful caller. Then in June 1990, Great Britain opened all stops to celebrate the one hundred and fiftieth anniversary of Hardy's birth as Trudy reported to me in a letter dated 10 October 1990:

> While you've been gadding about around the North Pole or some such place [I had been touring Alaska in my motorhome] I have been carried in my wheelchair, by four hefty male citizens up the many steps and into the Church which was full of folks who seemed to know the name of Hardy—then a little later I might have been found in Evershot Church with another crowd who seemed interested in the name. Bouquet of flowers sat on my lap was told I had beaten the Queen Mother who was a mere ninety years old.

Trudy as of this writing was ninety-three. The church she mentions is the parish church next door to Tower Hill. Though Trudy beat the Queen Mother to ninety-three, the Queen Mother outlived Trudy, living to be one hundred and one.

> Since June 2nd [she continues] Tower Hill seems to have been opening its doors to streams of pro-Hardyites. I tell 'ee professors and doctors of literature, music and everything else have climbed our little hill, saying We won't tire her—just to see her for a few minutes, though their ideas as to a few minutes did not mean just what they said! Well, I was going to say—they be quite common to I nowadays—instead of being dumb in the presence of such majesty we are now sort of "hail fellows well met" and I treat them like ordinary fellow beings and enjoy them and they have been happy here.

In the years since I had last visited her with Barbara and Rachel, Trudy had become confined to a wheelchair. No longer could she "run sprightly up the stairs" to fetch a remembered trophy. Diana, always the devoted daughter, had transformed the downstairs living room into a bed-sitting room for Trudy. However, though weaker in body, her wits and pleasure in people were as sharp as ever as the preceding excerpts show. She wrote me of another event that took place during the celebration of Hardy's birth:

> ...Do you remember the Yetties whom we saw at the B.B.C. place in Southampton on a beautiful sunny day years ago? Well, it seems we were quite interested in each other but the idiotic producer did not introduce us. They call themselves the Yetties because they live in Yetminster which is quite near us.
>
> They invited us to hear the launching of a new number of theirs for they are allowed to use Hardy's violin on loan from the museum in Dorchester. Someone also had and had repaired a 'cello which is supposed to have belonged to the Hardy family.
>
> Any way up we went to Dorchester—me in the old wheelchair and I was photographed by B.B.C. with Hardy's violin on my lap and the Yetties doing their stuff. But somehow...B.B.C. had too much on their plate to give us more than a quick run through when the time came. So no Hollywood!!!

Even though the television exposure had been brief, Trudy reported she received "lots of letters from folks I had known when I was young etc, etc." and one from an acquaintance who picked up the broadcast in Australia.

Further, in connection with the Hardy celebrations, there were revivals of some of the dramatic adaptations of his novels. On one occasion she and Diana journeyed "wheelchair and all to the lovely old Theatre Royal itself at Bath." They went by invitation to see Tess played by a youth company, age eighteen to twenty-two. She said she could imagine Hardy and Emma there when they were in Bath in their early days. She reported that the house was full, "interviews, cameras and flowers. Really felt as if I were a 'dame' or somebody!"

Sometime before that she had been also to Colfax School in Bridport to see another Tess. She said nothing of that performance but she had

> a lovely journey back mostly after midnight. We found two of "Tess" cows straying on the highway but managed to avoid them. Lovely moon and lights of towns as we bypassed them. And for a week following I told myself I am an old fool and should have stayed at at home.

The letter concluded, "So ends the celebrations of what would have been the old man's 150th birthday."

As 1990 drew to a close and Trudy's ninety-fourth birthday approached, I increasingly felt that I must see her again. I was living in Florida at the time with a companion who had never been to Great Britain, who had never met Trudy. I wrote to Di to ask whether Trudy would be up to a visit from the two of us, and it was Trudy who replied that two little bedrooms were waiting, they had room for a car if we had one, a great big welcome would be waiting also, and the longer we could stay the better.

Trudy's long letters continued to come. Her spirit was buoyant. Gordon Beningfield was still a mainstay. He had "rung up" recently to say he had another book coming out and that he had met the "Royals," would be bringing over a photo to share. She wrote,

> He gave us a picture of the painting he had done for the Queen Mother. She and the picture are in the photo. Can't aspire to such heights myself but a sister of George VI did come (incognito) to the Duke of York in 1929— so there!!!

In early March 1991, Mack and I flew to Gatwick and rented a car. She had a postcard an uncle had sent during World War II to someone in her family from a town in Kent. We did find the site of the postcard but not the information she was hoping for. From there we wandered through southern England, arriving in Beaminster the afternoon of March 8 for Trudy's birthday. We found her feebler than in my previous visit but just as keen and welcoming as always. Di planned the "birthday party" to coincide with teatime. We gave Trudy the small gifts we had brought, including a poem I had written for the occasion, called "On Greenfield Hill." Di presented her usual delicious teatime goodies with a birthday cake. We were the only guests for the event, and about all the excitement Trudy was prepared to deal with so soon after our arrival. I proposed to Di that Mack and I find lodging in a local inn, but both she and Trudy urged us to stay with them, and stay we did for two or three days.

For two or three days, a couple of hours in the morning and a couple more in the afternoon, I sat by Trudy in her wheelchair and we "remembered." Mack sitting in the next room, chatting with Diana as they knitted and needle-pointed, said later that for two days she heard, "I remember....Do you remember da, da, da? Everyone remembers...." Trudy recalled how, even after her marriage and with a baby daughter, she continued to act with the Hardy Players. "Oh, I loved to act," she said, and her eyes sparkled as she said it.

She told me, "In 1924 Mr. Tilley [of the Hardy Players] came to me with a message that Mr. Hardy would particularly like me to play the part of Tess. I was torn. My dear husband knew how much I loved acting and made no objection. So I said I would. I had to go eighteen miles twice a week to rehearsals. With my baby in my arms I traveled six miles by bus to Bridport, waited half an hour for the train to Maiden Newton where I had another half hour to wait for the train to Dorchester. That was 1924. I did not play Tess in London until five years later. By that time Diana was old enough to stay at home with her father, and I had rooms in London. When my six-month contract at the Duke of York Theatre ended, I was urged to take the play on the circuit, but I had promised my husband I would come home. I was missing him and my daughter very much. After nine performances a week, I was quite ready to return to Beaminister."

As I sat there by her wheelchair, we remembered the Yetties, we remembered the time she missed her bus to J.O. Bailey in North Carolina, we remembered her visits to Connecticut and her meeting my family. We laughed to remember how she hoped my twelve-year-old nephew and her twelve-year-old grandson would become pen pals. She must have known acting better than she did boys. We remembered the little book she once wrote about her memories of Thomas Hardy. Her granddaughter was currently editing it and anticipating publication.

"She'd better hurry; that's all I have to say, if I'm ever going to see it in print," Trudy commented.

Too soon our visit was over, and Mack and I midst hugs and come agains drove slowly down the lane from Tower Hill.

Trudy continued to write her three- and four-paged letters; visitors continued to make their way to her in her wheelchair. On March 8, 1992, I phoned to say "Happy ninety-fifth birthday." She had just finished her dinner with Diana and grandson Michael and his family. Her voice was clear; her attitude upbeat; her laugh contagious.

I had one more letter after that, the penmanship perhaps a little shaky, but the details still vivid as she described a visit from Gordon Beningfield. Then on August 8, 1992, the phone rang in my Florida home. The moment I heard Di's "Eve-lynn?" I knew the message.

"Mum died in her sleep last night. It was very peaceful. She was ready to go." The woman whom The Sunday Telegraph on February 11, 1990, had called a "living footnote to the history of English literature" was at rest.

All the principal newspapers carried her obituary; 150 friends and admirers came to the memorial service in the parish church.

One eulogist read numerous reviews of her sterling performance as Tess at the Duke of York Theatre in 1929. Gordon Beningfield spoke of her love of family, life, and the Dorset countryside. "She was so keen on the natural world," he said and proceeded to tell of a visit after she was confined to her wheelchair. They were talking of the beauty that abounds in Dorset when she said, "There's not much point in sitting here talking about it when it's all around us. Let us go and look at it."

"Just how are we going to manage that?" he asked, a bit perplexed.

"I'll get lifted into the car and away we'll go." And they did.

They drove to several favorite sites, many of which he had painted, and ended up on top of Edgarton Hill, where they sat and talked. Trudy recalled her memories of that spot, especially of picnics. "She had the ability to encourage everyone," he said. "I am a better painter of Hardy's Wessex because of what she helped me see."

Granddaughter Christine read what Grandma had once told her was her favorite poem, "Regret Not Me," which concludes,

> Mourn not me beneath the yellowing tree
> for I shall mind not, slumbering peacefully.

Trudy in dogwood time

On Greenfield Hill

You stood one day on Greenfield Hill
Mid dogwoods white and high
Where all rejoiced to hear the voice
Of Tess and Stacia Vye.

From Lewiston, Maine, to Lambert Castle
The days and years have passed
Since I first sought your Dorset door
With questions to be asked.

From steamboat dock to airport gate
I picture you at will,
But still I come most often back
To spring on Greenfield Hill.

Notes

[1] Thirty-six years after I talked with the young man from Slimbridge, a friend and I were making our way from Gloucester through Bristol to Llanidloes, Wales. I might have driven to Slimbridge, a village too small to be on our road map, without giving it thought, had we not come upon the name Peter Scott. "Peter Scott, bird artist," the young man had said. In the intervening years, I had developed a keen interest in birds, and the name Peter Scott gave me pause. We followed the signs to the Peter Scott Wildlife Preserve and spent the rest of the day watching and photographing Ruddy Shelducks, a Pink-footed Goose and Bean Goose, Red-crested Pochard, Bewick Swan, and several other exotic birds we could not find in any of our bird books. When my mind cleared, I wondered where the young man of the literature festival was today. I should have enjoyed telling him of our serendipitous day in Slimbridge.

Trudy and author